飲食精華

your Favorite Recipes

CONTENTS

INTRODUCTION

I compiled YOUR FAVORITE RECIPES after eight years of teaching over 2,500 students in many Chinese cooking classes. The students tested and tasted these recipes. Some were created by popular demand. Others were eliminated because of lukewarm responses. Still others were dismissed because they were difficult to perfect with limited home kitchen equipment. As questions arose the recipes were revised and edited for better understanding and implementing. Instead of presenting bird's nest soup, thousand year eggs or sea slugs to tax and test your taste buds, I offer simple-to-follow instructions and easy successes to please your palate.

My students are so thrilled with their accomplishments after a few lessons. Some typical exclamations that I hear are:

> "It's so easy when you know how!"
> "My husband was so-o proud of me!"
> "My guests were so-o impressed!"

On the other side of the cleaver, I hear,

> "But it took me all day to cut and chop!"
> "My kitchen was a disaster area!"
> "How do you do everything the last minute?!"

So, to make entertaining easier for yourself and to get the most out of this book read the front pages on preparation ahead and techniques for sautéing, deep-frying and cutting. There are helpful hints following each recipe to eliminate last-minute cooking.

Many hostesses feel they have to serve as many dishes as they are served when dining out Chinese style. If you follow the Chinese tradition, the greater the number of dishes you serve, the greater the honor you accord your guests. But, in this country where you are the hostess, the cook and the maid, compromises make sense. You can treat your guests royally with two entrées with steamed rice and wine, preceded by a couple of made-ahead hors d'ouevres.

1

The meal can be finished with a dessert. I always advise my students to feel comfortable with their dinner plans and not to go to extremes when entertaining. It's helpful and reassuring to test recipes on your own family prior to a big dinner party.

The following story illustrates my point. A student shared with me her plans for an elaborate feast for ten people. She had invited her husband's boss and some very special friends. I tried to convince her to cut down the number of entrées from eight to four which with hors d'oeuvres, wine and dessert would have been ample! But she insisted that she was familiar with all the dishes and felt absolutely confident about her big debut. (I lost sleep that weekend thinking of her, as I would have had a difficult time with the plans myself!)

Well, the following week she spoke of the evening, beaming all the while. Her dinner was a huge "happening." Her guests were wined and dined for three heavenly hours — punctuating their pleasures with "oh's" and "ah's." Between specialties she disappeared behind her kitchen door for ten minutes to make more magic, delighting her guests over and over again. Her husband could not praise her enough. The company lavished laurels on her for days after.

Then she finished her story, "Next week I'm having company again. The h--- with it, I'm serving barbecued beef-burgers and a salad!"

Simplicity is the key to entertaining.

3

IMPORTANT INFORMATION

CHINESE COOKING EVALUATED

Many people are discovering a whole new world of gastronomic delights in the Chinese cuisine. It offers endless varieties and combinations of condiments, foodstuffs, meats and vegetables. New approaches to everyday foods give them a regal air. Sophistocated use of seasonings transforms tired dishes into mouth-watering specialties.

Not only is Chinese cooking exciting, but it can be highly nutritious. Vegetables sautéed briefly retain their natural vitamins and minerals. Vegetable oils used in cooking are high in unsaturated fats. Butter, cream, cheese and sour cream, high in cholesterol which is a saturated fat, are not a part of traditional Chinese cooking. Health authorities urge us to use less saturated fats to reduce the hazards of coronary heart disease.

If you are trying to cut calories, a "Teflon" or "T-Fal"-lined pan used to sauté helps to reduce the amount of oil needed. Also, by subtracting starches such as noodles and rice and adding more meat and vegetables, you can diet without deprivation and have pleasure without regrets.

Most of these recipes can be made from groceries available in American supermarkets. Even if you are missing some Chinese condiments and foodstuffs, your recipes still retain their foreign accents and your method of cooking is distinctly Chinese.

I am often asked, "Are these recipes authentic?" The basic idea is. Food preparation in any cuisine is not stationary. It changes, improves and adapts to availability of foodstuffs, creative innovations and taste preferences. A good example is beef stew which has proliferated from the simple boiling together of meat and vegetables to endless variations and versions.

Most Chinese cuisine is easy on the budget. Buy vegetables in season and take advantage of specials in meat.

DO YOU NEED A WOK?

Everyone asks me, "Do I need a wok to cook Chinese food?" My answer is a positive "no" to the surprise of everyone and the disappointment of a few.

The wok is a metal frying pan shaped like a shallow salad bowl. The ones designed for restaurants have 24-inch to 30-inch diameters and are covered with high-domed lids. They are set deep into counters. The two handles, one on each side, meet flush with the countertop. Gas from below heats the entire wok and gives sufficient heat. It is an all purpose age-old pan of ingenious design, large enough to steam whole melons and to deep-fry whole chickens and small enough to sauté a dish to serve one.

For home use, however, the wok presents a completely different picture. A wok, 10 to 12 inches in diameter, comes with a 2-inch high ring on which the pan sits stably. The bottom is unable to lie flat on the burner and essential heat is lost.

For recipes requiring sautéing, high heat is absolutely necessary. To utilize maximum heat from the stove burners, you need a flat-bottom skillet such as a heavy cast-iron one or a heavy-gauge aluminum pan with a cover. A chicken fryer is a good example. Many beginning cooks have trouble with foods sticking because they do not heat the pans high enough to seal in meat juices. "Teflon"-lined pans are good for their nonsticking qualities. They peel, however, with repeated use on intense heat. A new cookware, coated with a nonsticking "T-Fal" lining, gives a longer life. Electric fry pans with one coil do not yield sufficient heat. They cannot compete with the coils of the burners on the stove.

THE CHINESE CLEAVER

The most indispensable tool in Chinese cooking is the cleaver. It has a wooden handle and a rectangular blade about 3 1/2 inches by 8 inches. It varies in size and weight according to the purpose for which it is intended. Besides cutting, slicing, chopping and mincing, it smashes garlic in the skin and freshly peeled ginger root. Its broad blade acts as a spatula for transporting food from the chopping board to the fry pan or to a dish. Its handle mashes beans and garlic as a pestle does. In a pinch, a heavy cleaver can substitute as a can opener for liquid foods by hitting its heel on top of the can to make slits.

The well equipped Chinese cook uses 3 or 4 cleavers of different sizes and weights. A light-weight one chops vegetables. A slightly heavier one cuts meats. A still heavier one cuts through bones of fowl and minces meat. The heaviest hacks through spareribs.

For your purposes in using these recipes you need one medium-weight, all-purpose cleaver to cut vegetables and meat, to cut through bones of fowl and to mince meat. (For my classes I recommend the number 3 cleaver. Ask for "sahm hoh gwong doh" in Chinese stores. It may also be purchased in gourmet cookery shops.)

You'll be surprised and pleased that you can master the use of a cleaver without difficulty. As with all tools you must learn to handle them to avoid accidents and to get maximum efficiency. So many of my students after using a cleaver a few weeks exclaim, "I'm lost without it. I use it for everything. How did I ever get along without one?"

Sharpen your cleaver with a carborundum stone, a honing steel, an electric sharpener or any gadget on the market. In using an electric sharpener pull the cleaver through steadily to sharpen the blade evenly. It's simple to give it a few whisks on a stone or steel each time you use it to keep it in tiptop shape.

To struggle with a dull knife is more hazardous than using a sharp one.

Most Chinese cleavers are made of carbon steel which holds a better edge than stainless steel. Do not put it in the dishwasher. Carbon steel will rust and a coat of food oil on the blade now and then will retard staining and rusting. Discoloration of the blade will not affect its function. Your cleaver is not an art object; it is a valuable workhorse.

Grip handle firmly close to the blade.

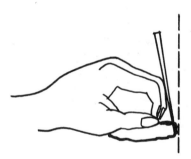

Hand holding food . . . Tuck fingernails under. Brace blade against knuckles which act as a cutting guide; slant blade away from fingers. Do not raise cutting edge above level of food. Motion is forward and downward.

To smash ginger or garlic . . . Scrape skin off ginger; leave skin on for garlic. Place on edge of board. Slam down hard close to handle where force is strongest.
Caution: Be sure your fingers clear the board!

CUTTING EQUIPMENT

CHEF'S KNIFE
is a must if you
don't have a
Chinese cleaver.
It can mince, slice and chop for all of these recipes.

PARING KNIFE
is handy for scraping the skin off ginger root and for stripping
the fibers from broccoli and
jicama.

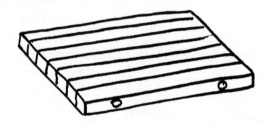

CHOPPING BOARD
The chopping board is the "silent partner" of the cleaver
which, despite its power, is crippled without its mate. A
board 10 by 14 inches will adequately serve all your heavy-
duty jobs. Leave the pretty laminated ones to decorate your
walls. Cutting on them is like walking on a slippery surface.

MAJOR CUTTING PATTERNS

The five major cutting patterns used in these recipes are:
1. ROLL CUT
2. DICE
3. SLICES OR BITE SIZE
4. SLIVERS OR SHREDS
5. GROUND OR MINCED

ROLL CUT
Bite size chunks about 1 1/2 inches long and 3/4 inches wide for root vegetables. For stouter vegetables, like potatoes, follow same idea but roll back 1 inch each turn.

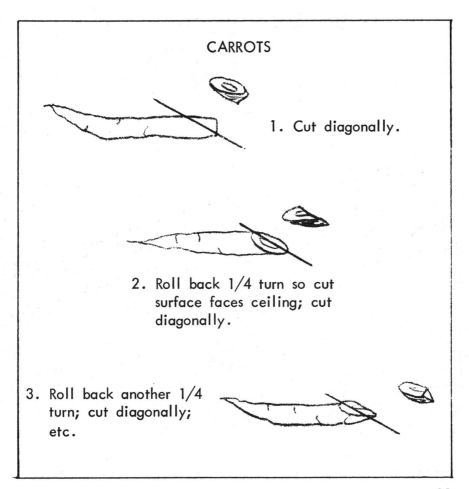

CARROTS

1. Cut diagonally.

2. Roll back 1/4 turn so cut surface faces ceiling; cut diagonally.

3. Roll back another 1/4 turn; cut diagonally; etc.

DICE
Cut into 1/2 inch cubes or sides.

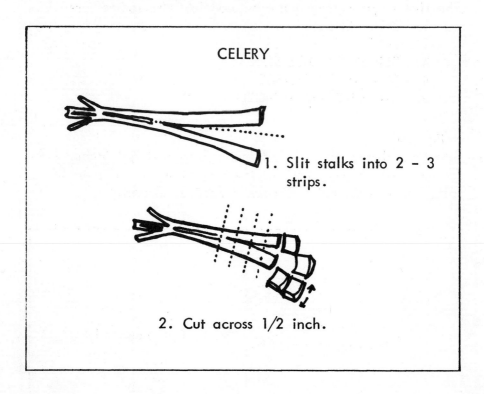

CELERY

1. Slit stalks into 2 - 3 strips.

2. Cut across 1/2 inch.

SLICES OR BITE SIZE
Approximately 1 inch sides and 1/4 inch thick.

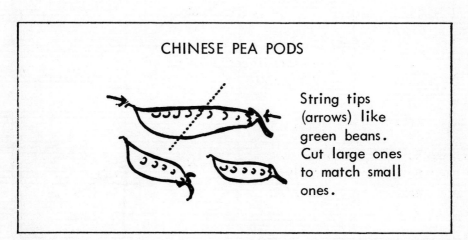

CHINESE PEA PODS

String tips (arrows) like green beans. Cut large ones to match small ones.

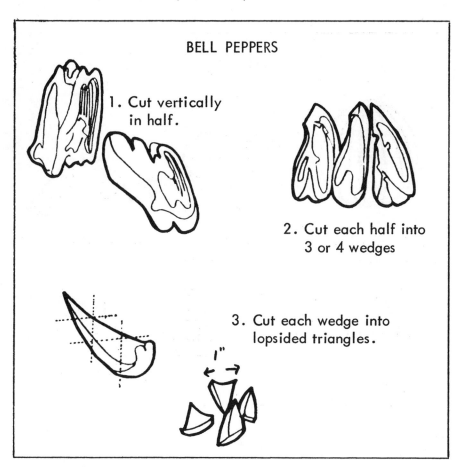

BELL PEPPERS

1. Cut vertically in half.

2. Cut each half into 3 or 4 wedges

3. Cut each wedge into lopsided triangles.

1"

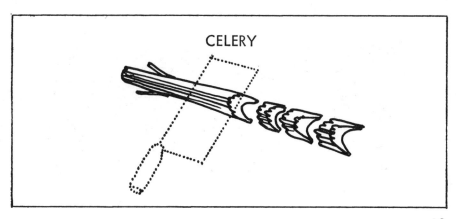

CELERY

SLICES OR BITE SIZE (continued)

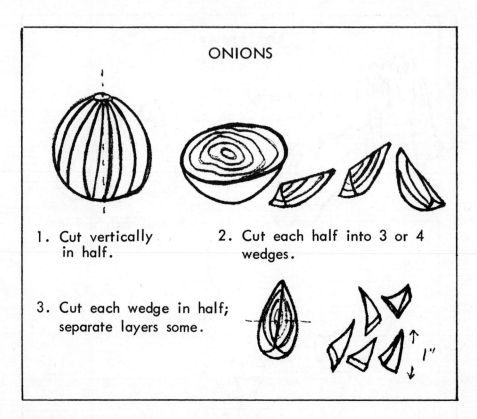

ONIONS

1. Cut vertically in half.

2. Cut each half into 3 or 4 wedges.

3. Cut each wedge in half; separate layers some.

1"

SLIVERS OR SHREDS
like cocktail picks.

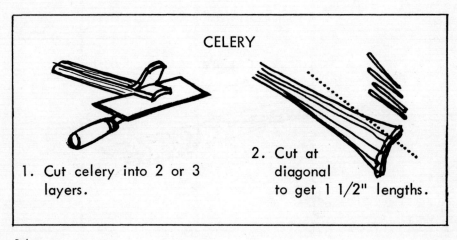

CELERY

1. Cut celery into 2 or 3 layers.

2. Cut at diagonal to get 1 1/2" lengths.

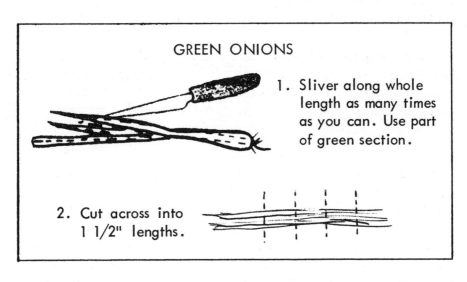

GREEN ONIONS

1. Sliver along whole length as many times as you can. Use part of green section.

2. Cut across into 1 1/2" lengths.

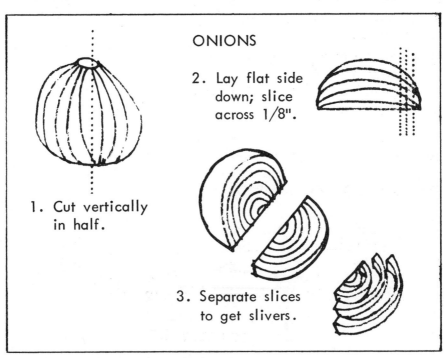

ONIONS

1. Cut vertically in half.

2. Lay flat side down; slice across 1/8".

3. Separate slices to get slivers.

GROUND OR MINCED
like hamburger or finer. For small amounts, use cleaver.

ALL YOU NEED TO KNOW
ABOUT STEAMING
AND STEAMERS

Steaming to cook foods is a method used as often as sautéing in the Chinese kitchen. It is a wholesome way to trim calories as very little oil is used compared to sautéing or deep-frying. There are many types of oriental steamers on the market, but you can easily improvise your own. See illustrations following.

First, you need a pot (with a lid) large enough to accommodate the vessel containing the food (see illustrations). Next, add water to the pot, the amount depending on the time required to cook the food. (Replenish water when necessary.) Then place a rack on the bottom of the pan to raise the vessel to prevent the water from boiling into the food. Buy a rack from a kitchenware department or use a heatproof dish, right side up with water in it to stabilize. Place the vessel of food on the rack, cover and bring water to a boil to steam. Time according to recipe when water begins to boil; lower heat to simmer to keep water bubbling gently. For steaming sponge cake, fun or dumplings let water bubble first before putting food in.

Note: A double boiler does not substitute as a steamer because it does not allow steam to circulate freely.

STEAMERS YOU CAN IMPROVISE

1. A fry pan (can be electric) . . .

. . . accommodates a shallow vessel.
Use for sponge cake, fun, siew mai,
or dumplings.

2. A soup pot . . .

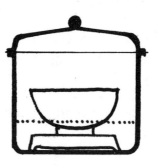

. . . accommodates
a large deep bowl.

3. A wok . . .

. . . accommodates a large
deep bowl or 2 cake pans;
first pan rests on rack;
chopsticks rest on first pan;
second pan rests on chopsticks.

THE ART OF SAUTÉING

The technique for Chinese cooking is the same whether you call it toss-cooking, stir-frying, or sautéing. The majority of recipes in this book favor this method of combining a dish of meat and vegetables with a gravy. Keep a few basic rules in mind and you'll have your favorite recipes at your fingertips.

Preparation

1. Cut up meat according to the style specified — chunks, slices, dice, shreds or ground. Season and mix. (Add seasoning directly to meat without premixing.)
2. Cut vegetables to match meat in bulk or shape or as directed. Separate them according to cooking time required.
3. Combine gravy ingredients.

Procedure

1. Sauté and salt vegetables, starting with "longest cooking" vegetables and ending with the "shortest cooking" vegetables. Remove from pan.
2. Sear meat to brown quickly, sealing in juices and preventing meat from sticking to the pan. Leave in pan.
3. Add gravy ingredients and stir till thickened, scraping bottom of the pan to clean. Return vegetables and toss lightly to mix.

Here you go . . .

SAUTÉING VEGETABLES

When you are confronted with a variety of vegetables and don't know where to begin, remember one rule. Don't overcook them. Using high heat sauté salted vegetables with enough oil to coat. A good rule on the amount of oil to use is to use enough to coat the bottom of your pan or your food. (So many students ask, "What is the glaze restaurants use over their vegetables?" It is just a coating of oil.) Then add a few tablespoons of water to

18

prevent scorching vegetables and cover, if necessary, to steam until translucent or half done. A little experience teaches you how long to cook each vegetable. For instance, if your pan is large enough and you have enough heat, you can start with your "longest cooking" vegetables such as oriental mushrooms and bamboo shoots. Then add your "next longest cooking" vegetables such as celery and onions. End with your "shortest cooking" vegetables such as pea pods and fresh mushrooms. Otherwise, cook each batch separately and remove from pan.

Whenever you are in doubt about the amount of time required for cooking vegetables it is preferable to undercook. They will cook some more when they are returned to the pan with the gravy ingredients. If you plan to keep the dish warm in the oven an hour or more, barely sauté the vegetables once around in the pan and allow them to finish cooking in the oven.

SEARING MEAT

Next, divide your meat into two batches or more and sear each batch with oil so it browns quickly without watering. Searing meat is crucial in determining whether you have a meat with a "barbecued" flavor or a meat that has turned to stew. Leave the meat in the pan when you add the gravy ingredients.

MAKING GRAVY

Next, stir gravy ingredients since cornstarch has a tendency to settle. Add mixture to the pan. Scrape the bottom of the pan to loosen any food that sticks. Return vegetables to the pan and allow gravy to bubble once around. Toss lightly together like a salad with chopsticks. Do not transform your creation into a messy witch's brew by overhandling! Although meat and vegetables are thrown together each retains its own characteristics while complementing the others.

The amount of gravy in a recipe should be enough to coat the food and a little extra. You may double the gravy so you can have extra to go over rice, but remember when you are serving three or four entrées all on one plate the gravies would run together.

Gravies should not be runny or thick. Cut down the liquid in your gravy ingredients if you have "watery" vegetables. If you cook ahead and hold food over in the oven remember that fresh mushrooms, asparagus and bean sprouts get soupy. It is easier to add liquid to thin a gravy than to add cornstarch to thicken it.

<table>
<tr><td colspan="3" align="center">Guide to Approximate Cooking Time for Vegetables</td></tr>
<tr><td align="center">Longest cooking
5 minutes</td><td align="center">Average cooking
2 minutes</td><td align="center">Shortest cooking
1 minute</td></tr>
<tr><td>Broccoli
Fresh green beans
Oriental mushrooms
Bamboo shoots
Carrots (need
  parboiling)</td><td>Celery
Onions
Green peppers
Green peas
  (frozen and fresh)
Bok choy
Nappa cabbage
Asparagus</td><td>Bean sprouts
Pea pods
Fresh mushrooms
Button mushrooms
Tomatoes</td></tr>
</table>

Cooking time guides are altered by:

1. Cutting patterns — slivers take less time than chunks.
2. Amount of vegetables sautéed. Heat is lowered in proportion to amount of vegetables added to pan.

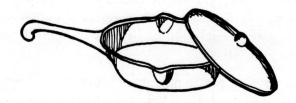

WHAT TO DO ABOUT SPATTERING

Spattering is inevitable when sautéing on high heat. Here are some hints to help you.

1. In between stirrings, cover the pan partially with a lid or a metal colander which lets out steam.

2. Take your pan off the burner for a few seconds to remove food from the pan.

3. Introduce your food all at once as in pan-fried noodles in Tomato Beef and Pan-Fried Noodles, p. 86, to cover the whole pan and you will not catch the spatter.

4. Use a long-handled spatula for sautéing, not a dinner fork!

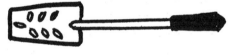

5. Wear a long-sleeved old shirt to protect your arms.

6. Use newspapers to line the floor if you are using the front burners.

ABOUT DEEP-FRYING

Deep-frying is a skill that requires practice for perfection. Even a novice can achieve delicious results if proper equipment and accessories are used, temperature guides followed, and safety precautions taken.

A DEEP-FAT FRYER
has the advantage of a built-in thermostat, but it is not necessary. A stable, heavy saucepan over the stove and a deep-fry thermometer serve the same purpose. (Candy thermometers are less accurate and break easily.) The shape and size of the pan used depend on the kind of food fried. For instance, for Egg Rolls use a skillet which can accommodate 4 to 5 egg rolls at a time. The shallowness of the skillet enables you to fish them out easily. For most foods, use a deep, heavy saucepan with a flat bottom. If your pan has a handle, push it toward the back of your stove.

ELECTRIC FRY PANS,
when new, are efficient enough for frying flat foods like Shrimp Toast and Teem Gawk. In my classes we find older pans often lose their efficiency. A morsel of food can lower the temperature as much as 20 degrees. We waste much time waiting for the heat to go up again.

ANY BLAND OIL
with a high-smoking temperature can be used for deep-frying. Salad oils do a good job. Never let your oil smoke as it will deteriorate. The amount of oil used depends on the food fried. It should be deep enough to allow foods to float freely around. To avoid bubbling over, do not fill your pan more than half full. Bubbling is caused by the moisture in the food. As the moisture dries the bubbling will subside. Continue to add food to the pan as long as the temperature is maintained and space is ample.

22

THE CORRECT TEMPERATURE

for most deep fat is around 375°. Without a thermometer you can determine this with a 1-inch cube of bread. Heat the oil. The bread will brown in it in one minute. Food should sizzle when introduced into the oil. The liquid is too hot if food burns on the outside, leaving the inside raw. If it sinks to the bottom, the oil is not hot enough, causing retention of excessive oil.

ACCESSORIES

make your job easier. A deep-fry basket contains small bits  of foods such as rice sticks and shrimp chips. It can be removed instantly when done. A fine-gauge strainer is necessary to skim loose food particles which, if left  in, will burn and contaminate your oil and food. Tongs and a long-handled slotted spoon are indispensable. Always drain food single-layer on paper towels. In frying large quantities of food, I put paper towels over thick folds of newspapers. The newspapers absorb extra oil and also serve as trays.

FOR SAFETY,

have a cover handy to cover the pan partially if food pops excessively. Use it in case the oil catches fire.

TURN OFF THE HEAT.

COVER THE SAUCEPAN.

DO NOT PUT WATER ON THE OIL!

DO NOT TRY TO TAKE THE PAN TO THE SINK!

TO STORE THE OIL,

cool it first. Then strain through a piece of cheesecloth or use a fine-gauge sieve. Refrigerate for longer life. Although you can use this oil again for deep-frying (not for confection after frying shrimp), it eventually browns and breaks down. I use up the oil in all my cooking, both in Chinese and American cuisines, so that I can use fresh oil each time I deep-fry.

NO-NO'S IN THE KITCHEN

1. Never cut on any surface except a chopping board.

2. Never use a small knife to tackle a big job; don't struggle with a dull knife.

3. Never use a small utensil to sauté. Use a long-handled spatula to avoid the spatter and heat.

4. Never scorch vegetables; add a little water to steam. Don't overcook vegetables.

5. Never put meat in a cold fry pan. Always sear it. Then turn down heat if necessary to cook through.

6. Never heat oil for deep-frying unattended; do not let it smoke!

7. Never follow directions blindly like a robot; understand the reasons.

HOW MUCH CAN YOU PREPARE AHEAD?

Your greatest concern is, "How do I manage everything the last minute?" The answer is, "You don't try!" All Chinese cookbooks agree that Chinese cooking requires a maximum of preparation and a minimum of cooking.

The most time-consuming aspect is the cutting and chopping of meat and vegetables, and this can be done the day ahead of your party. You can even season your meat, but cut down on the amount of garlic by half. Assemble your vegetables for each recipe on one platter; otherwise you may end up with your own brand of chop suey (not necessarily a bad thing).

Mix and jar your gravy ingredients and label them.

The day of your dinner remove from refrigerator a couple of hours to thaw gravy ingredients and meat before cooking. Sprinkle water over vegetables as they will have dried out overnight.

A couple of hours before serving you can sauté your meat and make the gravy. Put in a shallow casserole (heats faster) without refrigeration. Cover and rewarm in a 300° oven 20 minutes before serving time or set the food in a chafing dish. Sauté your vegetables as close to serving time as is comfortable for you (most of them take only 1 to 2 minutes) and toss them in with your meat.

Most deep-fried foods taste best when eaten right away, but most of us do not relish last-minute complicated or strenuous cooking so we settle for "second best" in favor of relaxed entertaining. You can deep-fry earlier in the day and rewarm in the oven. A frequent question comes up about the quality of deep-fried foods after freezing. To satisfy yourself, try putting some leftovers in the freezer and rewarm them a couple of weeks later and see if they meet your approval.

You are always your severest critic. So many students tell me, "My vegetables were not as crunchy as they were in class, but everything was cleaned up!" or "My Egg Rolls were a little soggy, but all my guests raved about them!"

To make it easier for yourself, include in your menu some "do-ahead" recipes such as Foil-Wrapped Chicken, Coriander Chicken Salad, Fried Wun Tun, or Barbecued Spareribs.

Steamed rice is not a problem and can be held over low heat. If you have an electric rice cooker you gain an extra burner on your stove. Plug it out of the way of your working area.

BE CREATIVE

The fun part of Chinese cooking is that it is so easy to "do your own thing." At first follow procedures rather closely. After a little experience you will understand the principles used and reject the role of a robot. You can add your own dimensions and give flair to foods with new ideas. (As in sewing, from one basic pattern you can create as many as six originals.) Meanwhile continue to dine in restaurants to get inspiration for different combinations of meats and vegetables (a good proportion of meat to vegetables is 1 part meat to 2 parts vegetables) and compare their final presentation with your own. Note especially the way vegetables are cut. Don't let your husband tell you that you can cook better than ----'s even if you can. You can always improve in some area just by tasting and analyzing someone else's cooking. After all, Chinese chefs go through years of apprenticeship before they qualify to serve the public.

Much of Chinese cooking is compatible with other cuisines. Certainly the techniques can be applied to all areas. I often hear such comments as "I now cook all my vegetables Chinese style"; "Your sweet and sour sauce goes great with my Swedish meatballs"; "I cleaned out my refrigerator and made chop suey"; and "I served a luncheon to the ladies of the Seventh Day Adventist Church using your recipes, omitting the meat." The Chinese method of cooking lends itself well to creative cookery.

TABLE SETTING AND SERVICE

In Chinese-style dining, the round table seating ten persons is convenient in terms of serving foods within easy reach of every diner. Each person is right "in the groove" with every other guest, seeing everybody and missing nothing. (King Arthur had the right idea when he seated his knights at a round table because it promoted a feeling of togetherness and sharing.)

Each diner is provided with a bowl for rice, a pair of chopsticks, a bowl for soup, a soup spoon, a plate for entrées and a tea cup. Teapots, serving spoons and small dishes for condiments are spread around the table.

For your own home entertaining do what is comfortable for you with function in mind. You can dramatize a Chinese dinner with typical Chinese dishes and utensils or you can serve it American style on a plate with a fork. (You don't eat rice from a plate with chopsticks.) The informal buffet is most popular because it affords the greatest ease for the hostess.

MENU

"What can I serve together?" is a common question. In the traditional Chinese dinner party the menu includes — besides soup(s) — different meats and vegetables, seasonings and methods of cooking to provide contrasting tastes and textures. Let variety be your guide.

Hint: Avoid two dishes looking alike. For instance, if two recipes call for bell pepper, rather than repeat, omit it in one recipe or substitute another vegetable such as Chinese pea pods or green peas.

SUGGESTED MENUS FOR EIGHT

Accompany with steamed rice and soup (optional). The first item after soup on each menu can serve as an hors d'oeuvre. Even if you omit one entrée from each, the menu will be adequate.

I

Egg Flower Soup

Fried Wun Tuns with
Cocktail Sauce or
Sweet and Sour Sauce

Barbecued Spareribs

Cashew Chicken

Mongolian Lamb

Fruit Compote à l'Orientale

II

Winter Melon Soup

Egg Rolls

Sesame Chicken

Broccoli Beef

Sweet and Sour Pork

Steamed Sponge Cake
with Orange Ginger Sauce

III

Bean Thread Soup
(with Chicken)

Fried Prawns with
Cocktail Sauce

Asparagus Chicken with
Black Bean Sauce

Beef and Chinese Pea Pods
over Snow

Egg Foo Young

Almond Velvet Pudding
and Sesame Seed Cookies
(see Almond Cookies)

IV

Bean Thread Soup
(with Abalone)

Deep-Fried Pork Cubes

Coriander Chicken Salad

Tomato Beef (omit noodles)

Sautéed Prawns
and Vegetables

Ginger Ice Cream
and Teem Gawk

TEA

Serve any tea that appeals to you. The two best known Chinese teas are Jasmine and Oolong which are available in all supermarkets. Making Chinese tea is no different from any other. Scald your china teapot. Put in the tea. Pour boiling water over and steep about 5 minutes. Serve. For most teas, steeping more than 5 minutes will bring out the bitter tannin. Experiment with the amount of tea to obtain the strength most pleasing to you. No sugar or cream is served with Chinese tea, but nobody says you can't.

WINES

Chinese wines are not true wines in that they are not distilled from grapes. The two popular ones are Shao Hsing, distilled from glutinous rice, and Mao Tai, distilled from sorghum. Both are potent liquors like whiskey. Japanese sake is similar to Shao Hsing and is served warm. You can serve your favorite American wines. They complement Chinese food beautifully. One famous restaurateur informs me he sells more Chenin Blanc and Grey Riesling than any other. Another popular one is Verdoux Blanc.

HOW TO MANIPULATE CHOPSTICKS

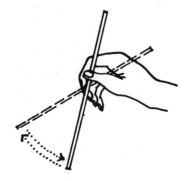

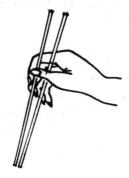

Hold top stick like a pencil. Practice bending your fingers as far as they will go. This is the stick that moves.

Slip bottom stick in the crotch of your thumb and fourth finger, bottom knuckle. The thumb pushes down and the knuckle pushes up, bracing the stick.

Tip: Keep your third finger away from the fourth! The top stick and fingers move independently.

MEASUREMENTS AND MISCELLANEOUS

2 CUPS MEAT
One pound of meat without any waste will yield 2 cups. Buy an extra 1/4 to 1/2 pound to allow for wastes in skin, fat and bones.

FLANK STEAK
is specified in these recipes because it is reliable for tenderness when cut across the grain. There are only two to each animal and demand often exceeds supply. Substitute top round or sirloin tip when price warrants. Flank steaks are sold whole and range from 1 to 1 3/4 pounds. Exact amounts are not necessary in these recipes. Adjust seasonings accordingly.

LAMB
Slices off the leg are leanest and the best buy. Chops have a lot of waste in fat and bones. Spring lamb has the most delicate flavor. Suggestion: When you buy a leg of lamb, "steal" a couple of slices to cook Chinese.

PORK
Any cut can be used—butt, loin, leg or tenderloin. Loin and butt are juicier because of higher fat content. When you see a lean and fresh butt or loin, buy it and cut it up in amounts with recipes in mind and freeze. When you see lean ground pork, grab it and freeze.

CHICKEN
Buy fryers 3 pounds or larger to get the most for your money. A 3-pound chicken will yield 2 cups of meat. Save carcass for broth.

WHEN IS MEAT DONE?
Cut open to check:

    Chicken — turns from pink to white
    Pork — turns from pink to white
    Sea food — turns from gray to white
    Duck — turns from pink to brown

CHICKEN BROTH
Boil together chicken bones with salt, dash MSG, ginger slices and celery to a rich consistency (gels). Freeze in ice cube trays; bag about 6 cubes to a package for gravies.

CHICKEN-FLAVORED SOUP BASE (p. 36)
may be substituted for broth for gravies. Follow directions on jar for dilution. Good also for boosting soups.

5/8 CUP LIQUID
called for in making gravies = 1/2 C + 2 Tables. (1 C = 16 Tables.)

GINGER ROOT SLICES
referred to in these recipes are the size of quarters.

CLOVE GARLIC
referred to in these recipes is the size of the last segment of your small finger.

ORIENTAL MUSHROOMS
Measurements need not be accurate. Use amount to please yourself or your pocketbook. Soak them 1/2 hour in warm water (about 1/2 C water for 1/2 oz. mushrooms) until they are spongy; discard stems; cut up according to recipe; save water for soups or gravies.

ALL MUSHROOMS AND BAMBOO SHOOTS
are referred to as "vegetables" for convenience.

"SIZZLE IN" SHERRY
is a term used in Chinese cooking. When your food is hot in your fry pan and sherry is introduced, it sizzles.

RECIPES SERVE 4 TO 6
Depends also on what else is on your menu and who your guests are.

FOODSTUFFS USED IN THESE RECIPES

In addition to familiar ingredients there are many which may not be as well known. Even so, they can be purchased at many supermarkets or oriental foodstores.

ABALONE, CANNED
comes in 1-pound sizes with whole pieces or big chunks to fit the can. Slice thinly and barely warm through; cooking toughens it. Save liquor for soups and gravies. Slice and eat cold as an hors d'oeuvre. Bits and pieces are not recommended.

ABALONE, FRESH
tastes bland compared to those canned. Pound prodigiously; slice thinly; sear quickly to cook.

BAMBOO SHOOTS
in tuna fish can size come in small thin slices; further cutting is necessary only when thin strips, dice or chopped is specified. Those in larger cans come in chunks and need to be cut up according to recipe. Buy cheaper oriental brands which save half or more. Transfer unused parts to plastic or glass containers and refrigerate. They keep about 1 week; change water every 2 to 3 days. Do not confuse them with bean sprouts!

BEAN SAUCE, SOYBEAN CONDIMENT,
AND MISO (Japanese name)
are the same. It is a yellowish brown paste or beans with a rich, salty taste — a perfect complement to bland soybean cake. It comes in cans or jars; the latter can be stored directly in the refrigerator. Transfer canned bean sauce to jars. Japanese miso, packed in plastic bags contained in plastic tubs, is stored as is in the refrigerator. It keeps 8 months or more.

BEAN SPROUTS

 come in bulk, packaged alone or combined with other vegetables labeled as "chop suey vegetables." Fresh bean sprouts are white and keep 3 to 4 days in the refrigerator before turning brown. Wash before using. Avoid canned bean sprouts; substitute finely shredded American cabbage.

BEAN THREADS

are labeled as such and are also known as long rice, cellophane noodles or Chinese vermicelli. They are wiry, transparent noodles made from the starch of mung beans. They are packed like a bundle of wires and are hard to separate. Use scissors to assist. Small 2-oz. packages are more convenient to use than larger sizes. Soak in warm water about 5 minutes to soften before cooking. Use in soups and stew-type recipes. They absorb a lot of liquid as spaghetti does. In a pinch substitute them for rice sticks, although they fluff less.

BLACK BEANS, CHINESE SALTED

are fermented, spongy, pungent beans packaged in 1/2- and 1-pound plastic bags labeled as "salted black beans" along with Chinese characters. Do not buy American brand black beans! Do not refrigerate. To insure against molding: Spread out and dry in the sun. Transfer to a jar with a tight lid. Salted black beans are lost without garlic. They make a perfect "marriage" — two strong characters who bring out the best in each other! Together they inspired the world-famous Cantonese Lobster. One of my students exulted after tasting black bean sauce, "The greatest contribution China made to the world is black beans!" "Lobster sauce" is a misnomer for black bean sauce used in Cantonese Lobster. When people refer to "Shrimp with Lobster Sauce," they mean shrimp with black bean sauce used with lobsters.

BOK CHOY

is a leafy vegetable sold in many supermarkets all year around. It has long, pronounced white ribs with medium to dark green leaves and grows to about 12 inches. Looks and tastes somewhat like chard. Pick those with lighter green leaves for tenderness. Hearts of bok choy (available in Chinese communities) are best. Delicious just sautéed with ginger slices, oil and salt. Discard yellow flowers.

CHICKEN-FLAVORED SOUP BASE

is a yellow gummy powder packaged in jars. Use to enrich soups, gravies, and sauces. Dilute with water according to directions and substitute for chicken broth in gravies. Bouillon can be substituted.

CHINESE CABBAGE (see Nappa Cabbage)

CHINESE MUSHROOMS (see Mushrooms)

CHINESE MUSTARD (see Mustard Paste)

CHINESE PARSLEY (see Coriander)

CHINESE PEA PODS

are also known as snow peas, China peas, sugar peas, or edible pea pods. These are not the same as American green peas in the pod! The price range is wide, depending on the season. There is no waste and they are light. Even at $2.00 a pound they are not prohibitive as 1/4 pound suffices for most recipes. Frozen pea pods may be substituted although they lack the crunchiness of fresh ones. If used, thaw, separate and blot dry. Use whole as they are tiny; sauté long enough only to heat through.

CHINESE SPICE POWDER (see Five-Fragrant-Spices Powder)

CHUTNEY
is a piquant, tantalizing relish made with spices and fruit; the most popular one is mango. One tablespoon goes a long way to spruce up meats and sauces. Comes in jars and keeps for months refrigerated. Many recipes use other fruits for chutney. (Write to Sunset Magazine.)

CILANTRO (see Coriander)

CORIANDER
(Chinese name Yuen Sai) is the same as Chinese parsley or

cilantro (Mexican name). You can grow your own from whole coriander seeds available from a supermarket spice shelf or cilantro seeds packaged and sold in the same section with other Mexican spices and condiments. Fresh coriander is sold in many supermarkets and also in Mexican food stores. It is a native of the Mediterranean area where missionaries brought it to Europe and Asia. It is enjoyed quite universally.

CORNSTARCH
is used to coat meat to improve its texture, as flour is used to dredge stew meat before browning. Also used to thicken gravies and bind foods. Gravies made with cornstarch are translucent; those with flour are opaque. It has twice the thickening power as flour. Many Chinese use tapioca starch interchangeably with cornstarch in the same proportions; the gravy is more glutinous.

CURRY POWDER
is a blend of spices such as cumin seed, coriander, turmeric, fenugreek, cardamon, red and black pepper. Brands differ in flavor (my favorite is Crosse and Blackwell). Some students who thought they did not care for curry were delighted to be converted. Perhaps their first introduction was overwhelmed by too much of a good thing. As with all condiments, when in doubt, use less rather than omit.

EGG ROLL WRAPPERS, -SKINS, -DOILIES
(Chinese name Chuen Guen Pay, for spring roll skin)
Available in the produce section in many supermarkets in 1/2- and 1-pound packages, about 20 sheets per pound. They are 6-1/2-inch dough squares made from egg, flour and water. They keep one week refrigerated; double wrap to prevent drying out. They freeze well 6 months or more if wrapped airtight. To thaw: allow 2 hours at room temperature, or the day before transfer from freezer to refrigerator. If they dry out put them in your refrigerator bin overnight to reconstitute. If badly cracked, they cannot be used for Egg Rolls, but can be cut up, deep-fried, and eaten like potato chips. In Honolulu wun tun chips are packaged and sold like potato chips. Since egg roll wrappers are four times the size of wun tun wrappers, they can be cut up to substitute.

FIVE-FRAGRANT-SPICES POWDER
is a blend of cinnamon, fennel, anise pepper, star anise and clove. Blends differ in taste as curry powder does. Use sparingly; a pinch goes a long way.

GINGER, CANDIED OR CRYSTALLIZED
is available in most supermarkets in the oriental foods or gourmet section packaged in cellophane bags, boxed or jarred with or without syrup. Oriental brands cost much less.

GINGER ROOT, FRESH,

next to soy sauce, is the most pertinent ingredient to Chinese cooking. Ginger root not only imparts a spicy, hot taste but counteracts strong tastes in meats. To season meats, the Chinese automatically speak of ginger, wine and soy sauce in one breath as if they were one condiment. (An addition to this inseparable threesome is often garlic.) Supermarkets which

carry it keep it in the produce section. Keeps at least 2 months refrigerated. It is still good when it dries out or changes color. If peeled and soaked in sherry, it retains its flavor for months. Freeze for longer preservation; cut off only the amount you need and return

unused portion to freezer; do not let it thaw as it gets pulpy. Ginger powder is not a good substitute as the quintessence of flavor and pungency is lost.

HOISIN SAUCE,

labeled as such, is sweet, and comes in round or rectangular cans. Many people call it red bean sauce because it is reddish (although it is made with yellow beans) or duck sauce because it is served with Peking Duck. Transfer to a jar and refrigerate. Keeps for at least 8 months.

JICAMA

(pronounced hee-cah-muh) is a Mexican root vegetable with a tough beige skin which strips off easily. It is round and squatty and weighs from 1/2 to 2 pounds. Chinese substitute it for water chestnuts and bamboo shoots because it is sweet and crunchy. Excellent shredded for American-type salads or eaten plain. Mexicans eat it as a fruit. Keeps 1 to 2 weeks in refrigerator.

LITCHEES
(also spelled Lychees or Litchis), canned, are round, sweet, juicy fruits the size of quarters with a white flesh the texture of grapes. They are shelled and pitted before canning in syrup. Combined (with their syrup) with other fruits, they lend an exotic taste to compotes and salads. They come in 20-oz. cans or smaller. They are natives of China. In the West they are grown in the Hawaiian Islands from where they are flown fresh frozen in the shell to Chinese communities in the summer months. Litchee nuts are the fruits dried in the thin reddish brown shells and are available in some super-markets in the gourmet foods section. They have the texture and color of raisins with a more fruity flavor.

LOONGANS
(phonetic translation means dragon eyes) are related to the lichees but they are smaller. They are natives of India. They are canned and dried and used like litchees.

MO GWA, JEET GWA, OR FUZZY MELON
is most available during summer months. "Gwa" means squash in Chinese, and this one is shaped like a watermelon. It weighs from 1/2 to 1 pound and has a bristly fuzz on a light green skin; peel before cooking. The flesh is white like a cucumber and cooks translucent. Its sweet taste makes it a great favorite.

MONOSODIUM GLUTAMATE (MSG), MEI-JING
(Chinese name), AJINIMOTO (Japanese name)
AND ACCENT
are all the same. It is cheaper to buy by generic name. MSG enhances the flavor in most foods, especially bland foods such

as soups and noodles. You may use less than recipes suggest
in view of the controversy that excessive use may be detri-
mental to your health. Commercial foods such as packaged
soups, gravies, sauces use it liberally.

MUSHROOMS, BUTTON
are used extensively in Chinese cooking. Substitute for or use
with dried or fresh mushrooms. Save juice for gravies or for
soups.

MUSHROOMS, DRIED, BLACK, FOREST,
ORIENTAL, DOONG GWOO (Chinese name),
SHIITAKE (Japanese name)
All are different names and varieties for the same delectable
fungus. They grow small as a dime or big as the palm of

your hand and are packaged in cello
bags. Most of them are cultivated in
Japan with the Chinese as their most
voracious consumers. Many Western
kitchens are discovering the distinctive
goodness of these mushrooms and have
introduced them into their own recipes,
giving them a new spark. Well endowed,
they lend much glamour to constant companions like bamboo
shoots without losing their own brilliance. You may need to
acquire a taste for them as they have a more pronounced
flavor and spongier texture than fresh or button mushrooms.
Use fewer rather than omit them; otherwise you would be
losing the best of Chinese cuisine! Give them half a chance
and you will be "hooked" with a lifetime habit. A bit expensive but worth every dime of it! Buy by the pound in
Chinatown food stores and save. Freeze for long life.

MUSHROOMS, FRESH
Rub and wash under running water. Do not soak as they
absorb too much water. Trim off black edge of stem (caused
by oxidation as in a cut apple). It is not necessary to peel off caps unless they are old. Some
cooks feel it is adequate just to brush off the

compost (sterilized) from the mushrooms without washing. If you are planning to hold food over, it is better to use button or dried mushrooms as they do not wilt and get watery.

MUSTARD PASTE, CHINESE
is powdered mustard mixed with enough cold water to form a paste the consistency of mayonnaise. Add a few drops of oil for smoothness and a few drops of vinegar for piquancy if desired. Use as a dip at the table alone or side by side in the same dish with catsup.

NAPPA CABBAGE, CHINESE CELERY,
SUI CHOY OR WONG NGA BOK (Chinese names)
grows to 12 inches with long white ribs and creamy yellow to yellow green leaves firmly packed. Choose lighter color stalks. Delicious sautéed with ginger slices, oil and salt or eaten raw in salads — American style.

NOODLES, DEEP-FRIED
can be purchased at the supermarket in the produce section. Chun King also puts them out in cans called "chow mein." Heat in the oven and use instead of pan-fried noodles for variety.

NOODLES, FRESH
are sold in the produce section in many supermarkets by the pound in plastic bags. They keep one week in the refrigerator and 6 months or more in the freezer. Allow 2 hours to thaw at room temperature or take from freezer and refrigerate overnight. A good substitute is Italian tagliarini, a fresh egg and flour noodle sold in most supermarkets. They are firmer, so scald them longer (1 minute) before pan-frying. If fresh noodles are not available, boil dry egg noodles (any kind) and brown slightly in pan with oil.

NOODLES, INSTANT
come in many Japanese brands and are packaged in single-serving cello bags usually with a packet of seasoning which is added to two to three cups of water. Bring the water to a boil; add your noodles and let them stand 2 to 3 minutes and you have instant noodle soup. You may drain these noodles and use them to substitute for pan-fried noodles or deep-fried noodles.

OIL

Use any bland vegetable oil which does not impart a taste to foods. Peanut and corn oils are de luxe but expensive. Use cottonseed, soybean, safflower, or a blend of any of these as long as it does not have a "fishy" odor when heated. Until recently cottonseed oil was plentiful and inexpensive as a by-product of cotton fiber. Today manmade fibers have decreased the demand for cotton fiber, consequently the supply of cottonseed oil has diminished.

OYSTER-FLAVORED SAUCE

is a thick, rich, meaty-flavored brown sauce bottled in 1/2- and 1-pound bottles. Use interchangeably or with soy sauce to enrich bland foods like noodles and boiled meat and for making rich gravies. It keeps 8 months or more if refrigerated.

PARSLEY, CHINESE (see Coriander)

PEA PODS (see Chinese Pea Pods)

PLUM SAUCE

often called duck sauce because, like hoisin sauce, it is commonly served with duck. Comes in 1-pound cans like hoisin sauce and bean sauce. "Dynasty" brand labels it as duck sauce. It is made from tart plums and spices and has a tangy taste. Transfer to a jar and refrigerate; keeps 8 months or more.

PRAWNS

are imported frozen from Mexico and Australia. When you buy them loose in the counter, they are thawed. It is not necessary to buy fancy jumbo ones as the price soars without any gain in quality. In recipes where prawns are to be minced or diced use smaller prawns to economize, although they require more work to peel. Cut costs also by buying the 5-pound block when on sale and divide it in

amounts for recipes intended. Thaw in a pan of cold water just enough to break up in chunks when you hit it over the edge of the counter. You can be assured of a "fresh" quality and not have to take chances with stale prawns. To improve the flavor soak in salt water (1 Tables. salt per pound) 5 minutes; rinse and drain well before using.

RICE STICKS

are labeled as such and are packed in layers like shredded wheat in rectangular-shaped 1/2- and 1-pound packages. They keep indefinitely like rice. They look like shredded coconut; do not mistake these rice sticks for bean threads which are transparent.

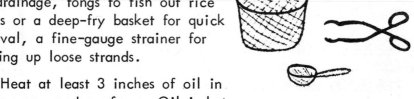

To fry: Have ready paper towels for drainage, tongs to fish out rice sticks or a deep-fry basket for quick removal, a fine-gauge strainer for picking up loose strands.

Heat at least 3 inches of oil in a saucepan or deep-fryer. Oil is hot enough when a strand of rice sticks dropped in sizzles and jumps to the surface (about 425°). Separate one layer of rice sticks into thirds and fry 1/3 layer at a time. Submerge completely in the oil; it will mushroom 5 times! Turn once if the top strands did not fluff; remove immediately to prevent burning; drain on paper towels. Make extra batches for your freezer. Heat in 200° oven 5 minutes to crisp, if necessary. Crumble before using. This is the "snow" called for in recipes.

SALTPETER, CHILEAN

is a curing salt butchers use to preserve meats like bacon, ham, luncheon meats and corned beef which gives them a pink color. It does not alter the taste of meats. Available in some butcher shops where they cure their own meats. Saltpeter from the pharmacy is not the same formula and will not turn meat pink.

SAUSAGES, CHINESE

are made from pork with or without pork livers. They keep like salami. Chinese love them steamed along with rice, which absorbs the juice from the sausages. Wash sausages (allow 1 sausage for one person) under hot tap water for 1/2 minute. Put directly on top of rice after water is absorbed. When rice is done, sausages are ready. Slice diagonally 1/4 inch thick and 1 1/2 inches long.

SESAME SEED OIL, CHINESE

is richly aromatic, amber and nutty in flavor, and different from American types, which are rendered clear and tasteless through the refining process, therefore not a substitute. Sesame seed oil is used sparingly (as a spice is used) to enhance mild foods or to modify undesirable odors and tastes. It is not used as a cooking oil because of its pronounced flavor. Keeps like other oils.

SHERRY, PALE DRY

is a good substitute for the Chinese rice wine which is five times more expensive. The purpose of wine (like ginger root and garlic) is to neutralize strong tastes and odors in meats. Gin or vodka resembles rice wine, but is also costly.

SHRIMP-FLAVORED CHIPS

come boxed in 1/2- and 1-pound sizes in assorted colors or plain white. They are made from shrimp meat and tapioca starch. Follow same instructions for rice sticks to deep-fry. Make ahead; cool and keep in airtight container or freeze. Serve like potato chips — good with cocktails.

SNOW PEAS (see Chinese Pea Pods)

SOYBEAN CAKE, - CURD, OR TOFU
(Japanese name)
Those sold by oriental food stores around here come in a 4- by
5-inch block soaked in water in a plastic carton with a red
or blue label. The blue label one is firmer and more suitable
for recipes used in this book. In Chinatown foodstores, bean
curd comes in different shapes and packages. Use the firm
kind for frying, the soft kind for soups. Before using, drain
well in colander; cut into 1-inch cubes and continue to drain
on paper towels until dry. Keeps 2 to 3 days refrigerated.
Sprinkle salt over to deter spoilage when it is necessary to
keep more than 3 days. Soybean cake, a product of soybean,
is a perfect food which contains all the essential amino acids
(proteins) to maintain good health. It is also high in vitamins
and minerals and low in starch. Babies allergic to cow's milk
are often fed soybean milk. Today, with so much emphasis on
natural foods with no preservatives, soybean cake should head
the list. Orientals prize its custard-like texture. By itself it
is rather pale, but develops personality when surrounded by
more robust friends like bean sauce and oyster sauce.

SOY SAUCE, SHOYU, OR SOYA
is the same. Use oriental brands which are naturally brewed
from fermented soybeans, parched wheat, salt and water.
American brands are instant soy sauces using hydrolyzed proteins
and are therefore not authentic. It is not necessary to dis-
tinguish between light or dark soy sauce in these recipes.
Light soy sauce is usually used for sea foods and soups; dark
soy sauce is less delicate and is used for heavier gravies.
Although soy sauce is salty, it is not a substitute for salt.

SUAY GOW PAY
translated means water dumpling skin. It is like wun tun
dough but is round. Trim off the corners from wun tun dough
to substitute. Handle and keep like egg roll dough.

SUB GUM
is a mixture of sweet-pickled vegetables and ginger in 1-1/2-
pound cans labeled as "mixed ginger" or "sweet mixed ginger"

with a picture of a variety of vegetables and ginger on the can. Good as an hors d'oeuvre. Once opened, transfer to jar and refrigerate; keeps like pickles.

TANGERINE OR MANDARIN ORANGE PEEL, DRIED
is very effective in removing strong tastes in meats like duck, fish, pork and beef. In making soups put in a piece the size of your whole thumb and boil together with bones. For other dishes, soak to soften and then cut up.

TAPIOCA STARCH
is used interchangeably with cornstarch. It makes a more glutinous gravy.

VINEGAR, CHINESE RED
is distilled from rice and bottled in 6- and 12-oz. sizes. Use as a dip at the table, like soy sauce and mustard paste. Good especially with deep-fried foods and chow mein; it cuts the grease. You can substitute malt vinegar.

WATER CHESTNUT FLOUR (WATER CHESTNUT POWDER)
is packaged in 1/2-pound plastic bags and boxed. Roll out lumps formed in storage with a rolling pin. It is used to coat foods for deep-frying. You may substitute cornstarch or tapioca starch, which is less expensive.

WATER CHESTNUTS, CANNED
bear no resemblance to their original goodness. They are nevertheless used extensively in restaurants because of their crunchiness.

WATER CHESTNUTS, FRESH
are commonly combined with bamboo shoots, mushrooms, pea pods or chopped with meats. Fresh ones are delectable with a taste between apples and coconuts. They enhance any dish and are worth the effort to get them. They are a special

treat as they are imported, highly perishable, expensive (90 cents a pound or more), and a lot of work to peel. They have a dark brown soft skin that peels easily. Do not mistake these for horse chestnuts which have a tough skin.

WINTER MELON
is a vegetable in the squash family, the size and shape of a  watermelon or smaller. It has a tough green skin with a white powder. Sold whole or cut up in chunks, it is used for soups and stew-type dishes. Bland by nature, it blossoms when it absorbs flavors from other foods.

WUN TUN WRAPPERS, - DOILIES, - SKINS, - PAY
are dough squares made from the same ingredients as egg roll wrappers, suay gow pay and fresh noodles. Handle and keep according to directions for egg roll wrappers.

零碎

MISCELLANEOUS RECIPES

WHAT YOU WANT TO KNOW ABOUT RICE

Q. How do you cook your rice so white and fluffy? Mine is so gummy.

A. Most Chinese cookbooks tell you to wash rice till the water runs clear. This washing removes the starch and talc. Talc is used in the final processing of rice to preserve it and to give it a finish. The more you wash your rice the whiter it will look, but you are flushing away vitamins and minerals. Your whole grain of rice is starch, so it is pointless to wash off the starch to cut calories. Fluffy rice is the result of using less water. The proportion of rice to water is about one to one in cooking 2 cups or less of rice. When you are cooking more than 2 cups of rice the rule changes, and you use even less water. See p. 53 on Steamed Rice.

Q. What kind of saucepan should I use?
A heavy-gauge aluminum or a stainless steel saucepan with a copper and/or aluminum bottom will conduct heat evenly. A Teflon-lined pan is excellent, especially if you don't want a crust. The level of your rice should come below half of your pan.

Q. Should I get a crust in the bottom of my pan?
A. The crust is expected. The longer the rice is held over heat, the thicker the crust.

Q. Can I salt rice?
A. Yes, although Chinese don't.

Q. What if the package says "Do not wash"?
A. Then don't, as rice is already sanitized and washing removes minerals and vitamins. For 2 cups of dry rice use 2 1/2 cups of water.

Q. What nutrients are in polished white rice?
A. Polishing removes most of the vitamins and minerals. The grain is mostly starch with little protein.

Q. What about converted rice?
A. This is rice with up to 80% of its vitamins and minerals retained by a process perfected during World War II. Follow directions on package.

Q. I use brown rice for its flavor and nutritional value. Can I cook it Chinese-style?
A. Certainly. After washing, soak the rice at least two hours to soften the "skin" and increase water by 1/4 cup, 2 cups rice to 2 1/2 cups water.

Q. Is rice fattening?
A. One half cup of rice contains about 100 calories. But you don't need butter or sour cream over it as you do with potatoes!

Q. Why is long-grained rice used in Chinese cooking?
A. Chinese prefer the firm texture of long-grained rice. You can use short-grained rice but decrease the amount of water. Use 1 cup rice to 1 cup water.

Q. Why do you prefer steamed rice to fried rice to accompany a series of entrées?
A. When a series of highly flavored entrées is served, plain rice goes well with the sauces and also neutralizes the taste buds. As in wine tasting, French bread is served between wines so you can better savor each one.

STEAMED RICE

2 C long-grain rice washed with warm water
through a strainer for 1 minute — swish
around with hand

Put in a 2-quart saucepan and add 2 1/4 C warm water;
cover partially (to eliminate boiling over); boil, without
stirring, until all the water is absorbed; there will be holes
in the rice at this point and no puddle when you tip the
pan. Stir once and cover; turn heat down to the lowest
point on your burner; cover and steam 1/2 hour. Take a
peek after 20 minutes; if rice seems too "hard" at this
point, add a few tablespoons hot tap water and finish
steaming. It is easy to correct "hard" rice, but impossible
to correct mushy rice. Fluff rice before serving. Two cups
of raw rice will yield about 4 1/2 cups cooked rice.

When you make more than 2 cups of rice, you use even
less water. Rather than keep the approximate one-to-one ratio
of rice to water, simply add water 1 knuckle above level of
rice. First wash the rice directly in the pan by swishing rice
around with hand and decanting water slowly. Repeat this 2
to 3 more times.

Over prolonged heating, a crust will form in the bottom
of the pan. You can make instant "sizzle rice" soup: Brown
the crust with 1 Tables. oil and add salt to taste; pour in
heated canned chicken broth. Break up crust before serving —
no waste and so delicious.

For company Sizzle Rice Soup, see p. 72.

To warm up leftover rice: Pour boiling water over rice
in the pan; drain; reheat on lowest heat for about 20 minutes,
or put into a bowl and steam.

FRIED RICE

- 1 C raw prawns — shelled, deveined, and cut up
    the size of peas; drain on paper towels
- 1 C barbecued pork — cut up same as prawns
- 4 C cooked rice on the dry side; break up clumps
    (put into plastic bag and squeeze from outside)
- 2 eggs, unbeaten
- 2 to 3 Tables. soy sauce
- 1 to 2 stalks green onions, chopped. Use all but
    withered parts
- salt
- oil for frying

In a red hot frying pan with 2 Tables. oil, sauté prawns until meat turns from gray to white; scrape to one side. Add barbecued pork, rice, eggs, soy sauce, green onions, and salt; sauté until eggs are done, adding more oil when necessary.

For variety and convenience, substitute other meats alone or combined: chicken, ham, shrimp, bacon, etc.; 1/2 C shredded lettuce or bean sprouts may also be added. Sauté raw meat first; add cold ingredients next, green onions and vegetables last.

Fried rice can be made ahead. Do not cook the eggs as dry. Put in casserole and keep warm in oven. If rice dries out sprinkle water or broth over.

A neighbor of mine thought Fried Rice was the greatest recipe for stretching the budget for her family of eight. She was telling me all the different foods she used to improvise and I said "fine" to all of them until she mentioned bologna! That is the dividing line between Chinese cooking and creative cooking!

EGG FOO YOUNG

Egg Foo Young is an omelet made with meat and vegetables, the combinations of which are endless.

> 1/2 pound raw prawns — shelled, deveined and cut
>   up the size of peas; drained on paper towels
> 1 small clove garlic, smashed
> 1/2 teas. ginger root, grated or smashed
> 1/2 C tender celery, slivered to match bean sprouts
> 1/2 C yellow onion, slivered to match bean sprouts
> 1/4 pound fresh bean sprouts, washed and drained
> 1 C fresh mushrooms — washed, drained, sliced (Cut
>   slices again in half for mushrooms big as half dollars)
> 1/4 teas. MSG
> 8 eggs beaten with salt to taste in a bowl
>
> salt, oil for frying

In frying pan on high heat using oil to coat food and salt as needed:
> Sauté prawns with garlic and ginger until meat turns
>   from gray to white; transfer to a colander with a
>   bowl under to catch juice.
> Sauté celery and onions for one minute; transfer to
>   colander.
> Sauté bean sprouts and mushrooms for one minute;
>   transfer to colander.
> Add 1/4 teas. MSG and toss prawns and vegetables to mix.
Draining vegetables is important to avoid a watery egg mixture.

Mix prawns and vegetables into beaten eggs. Starting on high heat, spoon mixture about 1/2 inch thick into frying pan with about 2 Tables. oil; golden brown and turn to brown other side, adding more oil if needed and turning down heat if necessary to prevent scorching. For family style, it is not necessary to turn the pancake whole; divide into parts easy for you to turn. Pile on a platter and serve with Egg Foo Young Sauce (recipe follows).

To make uniform pancakes: Use tuna fish or pineapple can rings for molds (discard 2 ends, oil rings inside before using). Put as many rings as will fit in hot frying pan or grill with oil; spoon about 1/4 cup mixture per ring; golden brown one side; remove ring; then flip to brown the other side. Be sure the pan is hot to start so the egg cooks when it hits the pan; otherwise it will run from your ring; turn down heat if necessary to prevent scorching.

Egg Foo Young may be made hours ahead or the day before and rewarmed in oven. Thaw from refrigerator to room temperature; place in 300° oven about 20 to 30 minutes, covering loosely with aluminum foil. Or sauté vegetables and meat and let drain in colander overnight.

Variations, any combination of these: cooked crab meat (superb!), barbecued pork, chicken, ham, bamboo shoots, water chestnuts, green peas, Chinese pea pods, oriental mushrooms. It is a good way to clean out your refrigerator and stretch your dinner simply by adding more eggs.

EGG FOO YOUNG SAUCE
(also Egg Roll Sauce)

Put into a saucepan the following ingredients; stir over high heat till sauce bubbles once around.

    1 1/2 Tables. cornstarch
    1 teas. sugar (optional)
    1 Tables. soy sauce
    1 Tables. plum sauce or Apricot Sauce (p. 77)
    1 C (cup — not can) chicken broth, regular strength
    1 teas. chicken-flavored soup base (optional) may
        be added for richer flavor

EGG ROLLS

Egg Rolls should be properly named Spring Rolls translated from the Chinese name Chuen Guen. A mixture of meat and vegetables is rolled up in a thin dough (see Egg Roll Wrappers, p. 38) and deep-fried, with or without a batter. There are many versions of egg rolls using different fillings and wrappers. Some are not deep-fried.

1 pound egg roll wrappers — package contains about
    20 sheets

This recipe makes about 10 egg rolls. (Freeze the unused wrappers.) Keep wrappers from drying out as you work by covering them with a sheet of slightly moistened paper towel. For filling, use same recipe as Egg Foo Young (p. 55).

Sauté prawns and vegetables; drain well in colander as directed; soggy vegetables make soggy egg rolls. (Omit eggs which are used when making Egg Foo Young.)

Half fill a 10-inch fry pan with oil and begin heating to about 375°.

Make batter (recipe follows) and pour about half of it into large pie tin. Wrap egg rolls as illustrated, p. 59. Do not wrap until you are ready to deep-fry. If filling is soggy, dough will disintegrate.

A 10-inch fry pan can accommodate 4 egg rolls at a time. Place egg rolls, 2 at a time, in pie tin with batter; spoon batter over top and sides quickly. Do not bother to cover every part of egg rolls and do not linger over battering — get egg rolls into oil immediately before they disintegrate. Pick up egg rolls on both ends with thumbs and index fingers very gingerly; lower gently into oil (oil is hot enough when a drop of batter sizzles in it). Golden brown and turn and brown other side. You may need to hold pale side of egg roll down to brown as it tends to flip upward. Remove with tongs and drain on paper towels. Cut diagonally with cleaver into fourths.

Transport in original shape to platter. For picnic-style, leave whole and eat with fingers like a taco. Serve with Egg Roll Sauce (p. 56), soy sauce, or mustard paste (p. 42).

May be refrigerated or frozen after deep-frying. To reheat: Thaw to room temperature; warm, single-layer and uncovered, in 300° oven 20 to 30 minutes. For freezing more than 1 month, use barbecued pork instead of prawns in the filling.

Egg Roll Filling #2

Shred like cocktail picks:
 2 1/2 C bamboo shoots
 2 stalks celery
 1/4 C oriental mushrooms, reconstituted first
 2 C barbecued pork

In hot fry pan salt and sauté bamboo shoots, celery and mushrooms with 4 Tables. oil for 1 minute; add 4 Tables. water; cover and steam until water is dried out — about 5 minutes. Add pork, dash MSG, and mix; remove from heat; cool before wrapping. Enough filling for about 10 egg rolls. Deep-fry with or without batter.

EGG ROLL BATTER

Make just before deep-frying.   For 10 egg rolls:
 1 C Bisquick
 1 C cornstarch
 1 C ice water, approximately; add slowly near end.
    (Ice water keeps the batter cold. When the cold
    batter hits the hot oil it fluffs more.)

Mix together lightly; leave lumps in. Consistency should be like pancake batter or slightly thinner. A thicker batter makes a thicker crust. Batter may be omitted to cut down calories.

TO SHAPE EGG ROLLS

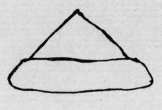

1. Position dough like a diamond. Spread 1/2 C or more filling on lower section of dough as shown.

2. Tuck bottom corner under filling and roll firmly; slightly pass left and right corners.

3. Fold left and right corners, forming leak-proof square corners; apply batter with fore-finger on edges as shown.

4. Roll and seal.

MEAT BUNS (BOW – rhymes with "wow")

A bow is a Chinese sandwich with different kinds of meat fillings such as pork, beef, and chicken with vegetables. Some have sweet fillings made with sweetened bean paste or lotus seed paste. The following uses meat and vegetables.

Filling, cut up the following into pea size:
    1 1/2 C raw chicken (omit skin) or pork
    1/2 C oriental mushrooms — reconstituted in 1/2 C
        warm water, or 1 C fresh mushrooms
    1 C of all or at least 2 of these: water chestnuts,
        bamboo shoots, celery, jicama (total = 1 C)
    1 whole green onion

Seasoning, combine:
    2 Tables. soy sauce
    1 Tables. sherry
    1 teas. sugar
    1 teas. cornstarch, or 2 teas. if fresh mushrooms are used
    2 Tables. water from soaking mushrooms, or plain water
    dash MSG

Dough:
    2 loaves of frozen bread dough (Bridgford's or Rhodes)
        thawed. Cut each loaf with cleaver in half length-
        wise and then each half into 8 even pieces. Flour
        your cleaver if dough sticks. Cover dough with
        damp towel to prevent drying out and crusting.

    Sesame seeds

Salt and sauté filling ingredients with 2 to 3 Tables. oil until meat is done. Add seasoning and stir till thickened, adding more cornstarch if necessary. Set aside to cool. Meanwhile, lightly oil 2 baking pans and preheat oven 375°.

Shape dough into balls and stretch into 3- to 4-inch rounds using a minimum of flour to prevent sticking to hands. Hold dough in left hand; put about 1 rounded Tables. or more of filling in the center without getting any on the edges. With your right hand, pinch tightly together 2 opposite

60

edges; round out bun; brush a little oil on top of bun; roll top of bun in sesame seeds; place bun seam side down on baking pan; leave at least 1/2-inch space between. Cover with dish towel; put in warm spot and let dough rise. Follow instructions on package of dough. Bake about 15 minutes 375° till golden. These buns are about 2 inches in diameter when baked.

Frozen bread dough closely resembles the Chinese dough except the latter is sweeter. You can knead in 4 Tables. sugar to each loaf of frozen dough after thawing.

Refrigerated biscuits (2 to 3 tubes) may be used instead of frozen bread. Stretch dough into 3-inch rounds and fill the same way (1 biscuit per bun). No raising of dough is needed.

Chinese-style buns are made as big as the palm of your hand and are more dough than filling. You can be as generous with the filling as you want as long as you don't puncture the dough. The original Chinese buns are steamed (put each bun on a 2-inch square white paper and steam 15 minutes; omit sesame seeds). The baked version is featured in many bakeries and restaurants today.

Buns may be rewarmed: Sprinkle water over, cover with foil; warm in 300° oven 20 minutes.

BARBECUED PORK BUNS (CHA SIEW BOW)

Make Barbecued Pork (p. 95), reserving marinade until last 5 minutes of baking and then adding to pork. Cool, dice into 1/4-inch cubes to get 2 cups, using fatty portions. Measure 1/4 C of drippings from pan — if drippings have dried out, add water to pan.

Add to drippings:
   1 teas. cornstarch
   1 teas. soy sauce
   1 teas. sherry
   1 teas. sugar

Sauté with salt and 1 Tables. oil:
   1/4 C celery, diced
   1/4 C onions, diced

Add the drippings mixture; stir till thickened. Mix with pork. This amount of filling is enough for 2 loaves of bread cut into 16 pieces. Follow same directions as for meat buns. Leftover barbecued pork can be used for other recipes.

SIEW MAI (A Steamed Dumpling)

A dumpling is meat and vegetables wrapped with a dough (suay gow pay) like wun tun dough except that it is round. There are many versions of steamed dumplings with many variations of meat fillings. This one is open-faced and shaped like a narrow cupcake. They are usually served as one of a myriad of pastries (diem sum) to accompany a tea luncheon. They are also sold in Chinatown shops specializing in tea pastries. You can serve them as another entrée or as an hors d'oeuvre. Two fillings are given.

Filling #1, using pork and prawns:

Dice first and mince together the following:
    1 C lean pork
    1 C prawns
    1/2 C bok choy
    1 whole green onion

Put into a bowl, add and mix:
    1 Tables. cornstarch
    1 Tables. soy sauce
    1 Tables. dry sherry
    1 teas. sesame oil
    1/4 teas. MSG
    1 teas. salt

Filling #2, using ground beef and dried cuttlefish (comes in 1-oz. cello bags — sold as snacks):

Mince together:
    1/4 C (1 oz.) dried cuttlefish
    1/2 C bamboo shoots, jicama or water chestnuts
    1/4 C oriental mushrooms, reconstituted first
    1 whole onion
    1 piece dried tangerine peel, the size of your thumb;
        soak 1/2 hour in hot water first

Put into a bowl, add and mix:
    1 3/4 C lean ground beef
    1 1/2 Tables. cornstarch
    2 Tables. sherry
    1 Tables. oil
    1/4 teas. sesame oil
    1 teas. salt
    1/4 teas. pepper
    dash MSG

Have ready for each recipe:
    24 suay gow pay (p. 46), or round off wun tun wrappers
    2 round cake pans, lightly oiled

    Wrap and shape as illustrated (p. 64).

TO SHAPE SIEW MAI

Spoon 1 Tables. of filling in center of suay gow wrapper. Use right thumb and index finger to form a circle to shape siew mai into cylinder 1 1/2 inches tall and 1 inch wide. (Think of a cupcake in paper.) Do not attempt to pleat evenly. Pack in filling with left hand in direction of arrows.

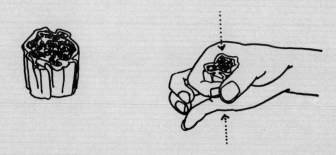

Oil each siew mai on the outside and lay 12 or more in a cake pan and steam 10 minutes or until dough turns translucent. May be made ahead, refrigerated or frozen. Thaw and resteam.

Use . . .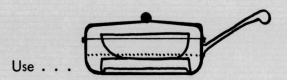

. . . or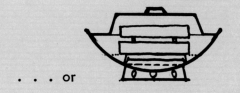

GOW JEE (A Steamed Dumpling)

This is another tea pastry (diem sum).
It is shaped like a turnover.

Filling, cut up first and mince together:
1/2 C pork
1/2 C prawns
1/2 C fresh water chestnuts or jicama
2 green onions

Put in a bowl and add:
1 Tables. soy sauce
1 Tables. sherry
1 Tables. oil
1/2 teas. sesame oil
1/4 teas. MSG
2 teas. cornstarch
salt to taste

Dough:
Bring 7/8 C water to a boil; turn off heat; add quickly
1 C wheat starch (comes in 1-pound bags and labeled as
such; can be purchased in oriental food stores); mix together
vigorously with wooden spoon until ball forms; cover to steam
for 2 minutes. Knead dough for 2 minutes, using more wheat
starch if necessary to prevent sticking to hands. Shape into
long roll about 1 1/2 inches in diameter. Slice across 1/4
inch thick, about 4 at a time; cover with hot damp cloth to
keep it pliable. Return uncut roll to saucepan and cover.
Roll out each round lightly, using a minimum of wheat starch.
Put about one rounded teaspoon filling in center; fold over
like turnovers; pinch edges together to seal. Brush oil over
each dumpling and place 12 in lightly oiled cake pan,
leaning one over another. Have water boiling in steamer;
cover and steam 15 to 20 minutes. Meanwhile finish shaping
the dumplings using second pan. You can steam 2 pans at the
same time if you have a 12-inch wok.

Can be prepared ahead and resteamed.

DEEP-FRIED WUN TUNS

Wun tuns are made with bits of meat wrapped in thin 3-inch dough squares. They are either deep-fried or boiled and put into soups. There are different fillings; this one is commonly used.

1 pound wun tun wrappers (p. 48)

Filling, cut up first and mince like paste the following:
3/4 C raw pork, any cut
3/4 C raw prawns
1 whole green onion
1 teas. or more chopped fresh coriander (optional)

Put into a bowl and mix with it:
1 Tables. soy sauce
1 Tables. dry sherry
1 teas. sesame oil
dash MSG
salt and pepper to taste

Wrap as illustrated, using only 1/4 teas. filling (the size of a lima bean). Do not be generous with the filling or the pork will not cook through by the time the dough turns golden. If you have to lower the heat to cook the pork through, the dough will absorb too much oil.

Deep-fry in 2 inches of oil at 375° with the meat side down first. Fry till golden; turn and golden brown the other side — takes less than 2 minutes. Drain single-layer on paper towels. Cut open to check for doneness. If filling is raw and the dough is already browned, loosely cover with foil and finish cooking in the oven 300° for 10 to 15 minutes.

Serve warm as hors d'oeuvres with Sweet and Sour Sauce (p. 116) or Cocktail Sauce (p. 116). As an entrée, use deep-fried wun tuns to substitute for pork in Sweet and Sour Pork recipe (p. 96). This is a popular luncheon fare.

To make ahead: Wrap and refrigerate overnight or freeze. Store without crowding to avoid sticking together. Use wax paper between layers. Tupperware boxes are good. You can go one step further by deep-frying them and then refrigerate or freeze. To rewarm, thaw to room temperature first, lay single-layer, uncovered, in 300° oven 10 to 15 minutes.

Variation: Use beef or chicken.

TO WRAP WUN TUNS

1. For Deep-Fried Wun Tuns, put 1/4 teas. filling on lower corner of dough; for Soup Wun Tuns, use 1/2 teas.

2. Roll up to left and right corners; put dab of filling on right. Bring 2 corners down.

3. Bring bottom of left corner on top of right; press to seal.

WUN TUN SOUP

Wrap wun tuns the same way as for deep-fried wun tuns (p. 67), but you can be more generous with the filling, using 1/2 teas. per wrapper. Allow 3 wun tuns per serving if this is part of a many-course dinner.

Soup for 4 to 6:

Put the following ingredients in a 2-quart saucepan; simmer 5 minutes:

    2 cans (11 oz. each) regular-strength chicken broth
    1 slice ginger root
    3 to 4 oriental mushrooms, the size of quarters,
        reconstituted and then diced
    4 oz. can sliced mushrooms, undrained
    1/4 C bamboo shoots or water chestnuts, diced

Just before serving, add:

    1/4 C frozen green peas or 1/4 C bok choy, cut up
        the size of your whole thumb; simmer 1 minute

Fill a 3-quart pot 3/4 full with water and 1 Tables. salt and bring to a boil. Release wun tuns (3 per person) and boil 1 more minute after they float. When water is rapidly boiling wun tuns tumble; remove pan from stove an instant and you can tell if they float. Scoop them up with a slotted spoon into individual serving bowls or a large soup tureen. Garnish with shredded barbecued pork or ham. Ladle ready-made soup over.

At the table, accompany with a soy sauce dip, individual or "one-for-all," to which chopped green onions, chopped coriander leaves, a few drops of sesame oil, and pepper have been added. The proper way to season wun tuns when individual dips are provided: Pick up wun tun with spoon in left hand, take chopstick with the right and dip into soy sauce, then onto wun tun. Or, if a "one-for-all" dip is used, accompany it with a small spoon and pass the dip around. If plain soy sauce is preferred, pass the dispenser around. Never pour soy sauce directly in your soup or you will wonder why you need gallons of tea to quench your thirst later! The reason wun tuns are not cooked directly in the soup is they make the soup messy and starchy.

Chinese do not eat wun tun soup as a prelude to a dinner. It is served for luncheons or midnight snacks. A whole lunch can be made from wun tun soup. Allow 10 to 20 per person. For serving a large quantity, put into soup tureen and ladle out at the table. Popular companions to wun tun soup are chow mein and chow fun.

You can make your own chicken broth from scratch. Boil together chicken and pork bones with salt, a few slices ginger root, 1 piece tangerine peel the size of your whole thumb, 2 stalks celery, 2 whole green onions; simmer 1 hour. Skim off fat, add 1/4 C sherry for 2 quarts broth. If soup needs a booster, add chicken-flavored soup base.

Soup can be made days ahead and refrigerated. Wun tuns can be wrapped and refrigerated one day ahead or frozen.

SUAY GOW (means Soup Dumplings)

Suay Gows are cousins to Soup Wun Tuns. They are eaten for lunch or midnight snack.

1/2 pound suay gow pay (p. 46)

Filling, cut up first and mince together the following:

    1/2 C pork
    1/2 C prawns
    1/4 C jicama (or fresh water chestnuts)
    1/4 C bok choy
    1/4 C oriental mushrooms, reconstituted
    1 whole green onion
    1 Tables. coriander (optional)
Put into a bowl; add:
    1 Tables. cornstarch
    1 Tables. soy sauce
    1 Tables. sherry
    1/2 teas. sesame oil
    salt and pepper
    dash MSG

Prepare a recipe for soup and soy sauce dips as used for wun tun (p. 68).

Put 1 Tables. filling evenly on half of suay gow pay. Fold over, press to seal. (The filling is sticky.) You have a turnover. Makes about 2 1/2 dozen.

Cook and serve like wun tun.

TURKEY SOUP (FAW GAI JOOK)

In an 8-quart pot, put:
    1 turkey carcass (10-pound bird), break up to fit pot
    1 C rice, wash first
    3 quarts water
    dried turnip (Chinese name choong choy), bulk the size
        of a walnut
    1 piece dried tangerine peel, size of your whole thumb
    salt

Bring to a boil, simmer until rice disintegrates and soup thickens to the consistency of split pea soup—about 2 hours.

Remove bones, turnip, tangerine peel and discard. Return meat from bones to soup; shred first.

Add 1/2 teas. sesame oil to soup.

At the table, serve with soy sauce to which green onions, coriander leaves and pepper have been added. Use sparingly to flavor soup.

Potato chips crumbled over soup are delicious.

Variations: Add ham bone, 1/2 C raw peanuts to pot to simmer with carcass.

For larger carcasses, increase water and rice accordingly.

Because of its thick consistency, turkey soup is served for breakfast like a hot cereal or for lunch or midnight snack.

SIZZLE RICE SOUP

When you make Steamed Rice (p. 53), a crust will form in the bottom of the pan. The longer the rice is held over heat, the thicker the crust will form. A crust 1/8-inch thick is desirable. After standing a day or two at room temperature, the crust will shrink away from the pan. Remove it in large pieces. Refrigerate or freeze until ready to use. This is deep-fried, broken up, and plunged into hot soup just before serving.

Have ready and heating:
> soup from Wun Tun Soup recipe (p. 68), but omit wun tuns and use frozen green peas

Heat 2 inches oil to 400°; deep-fry pieces of rice crust until golden; remove with strainer; put in warmed dish.

Ladle soup in tureen; take to table with rice crust. Submerge crust in soup and break up with long-handled spoon. Rice will sizzle, sing or crackle for you and delight your guests. This is a fun way to "break the ice." It is probably easiest if one person serves and the guests pass the bowls.

A pot with a 7-inch diameter will give enough rice crust for 1 recipe, which serves 4 to 6.

If you have an electric pot to heat soup at the table, all you need do is deep-fry your rice crust and take it to the table.

EGG FLOWER SOUP

Into 2-quart saucepan, put:
> 2 cans (11 oz. each) regular-strength chicken broth
> 1 Tables. sherry
> 1 can (4 oz.) button mushrooms, sliced (and juice)
> 1/2 C frozen green peas

Bring to a boil; add one slightly beaten egg and swirl once around, describing a big "S" with spoon or chopsticks; remove from heat.

72

MELON SOUP

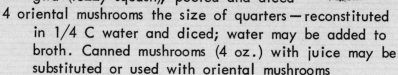

Into 2-quart saucepan, put:
    2 cans (about 11 oz. each)
        regular-strength chicken broth
    1 Tables. sherry
    1 slice fresh ginger root
    1/2 pound winter melon or one small mo
        gwa (fuzzy squash), peeled and diced
    4 oriental mushrooms the size of quarters — reconstituted
        in 1/4 C water and diced; water may be added to
        broth. Canned mushrooms (4 oz.) with juice may be
        substituted or used with oriental mushrooms
Cover and simmer until melon is translucent — takes about
20 minutes or more. Garnish with minced cooked ham and
chopped green onions. Serves 4.

BEAN THREAD SOUP

Have ready:
    about 1/2 C bean threads; soak 5 minutes in warm water
        to soften; cut into 2-inch lengths. (You will have a
        hard time separating bean threads as they are like a
        bundle of wires; use scissors to assist.)
    about 1/2 C raw chicken; dice the size of peas and mix
        with 1 teas. soy sauce, 1 teas. cornstarch and salt
        to taste
Into a 2-quart saucepan, put:
    2 cans (11 oz. each) regular-strength chicken broth
    1 Tables. sherry
    1 can (4 oz.) button mushrooms, sliced (and juice)

Bring to a boil; add bean threads and chicken and bring
back to a boil; cook 2 minutes more or until chicken is done.
Garnish with shredded barbecued pork or cooked ham and
chopped green onion.
    Variation: 1/2 C shredded canned abalone may be substi-
tuted for chicken. Add to soup just before serving without
boiling.

WINTER CHAFING DISH OR MONGOLIAN POT
(DA BING LOW)

Needed for cooking at table:
>   electric fry pan, long-handled slotted
>   spoons, extension cord.

Food for 4:
>   1 46-oz. can chicken broth with 3 slices ginger root

Prepare:
>   1/2 pound flank steak, slice (p. 85) and mix with:

3 slices ginger root
1 1/2 teas. cornstarch
1 1/2 teas. soy sauce
2 teas. oil
salt to taste

1 large whole chicken breast — bone and cut up the
>   size of your whole thumb; remove skin if desired;
>   mix with same ingredients as for flank steak (keep
>   in separate dish)

1/2 pound large prawns — shell, devein, butterfly, wash
>   and drain, mix with:

1 1/2 teas. cornstarch
2 teas. oil
salt to taste

1/2 pound or more clams — scrub and rinse

1 jar oysters — drain and discard liquid; put in a bowl
>   and add:

1 Tables. lemon juice
2 Tables. grated ginger root
salt to taste

1 can abalone, cut 1/4-inch thick and 1-inch x 1-1/2-
>   inch slices; add liquor to broth. Or use:

fresh abalone, pound prodigiously, slice the same.

74

1/2 block soybean cake or more — drain, cut up into
    1-inch cubes

Nappa cabbage (about 1 pound) — wash, cut up into
    1-inch widths, or 1 bunch spinach — remove stems,
    wash free of sand

Make garlic oil:
    Lightly brown 2 cloves smashed garlic in 3 Tables. oil
    (to be added to dipping sauces). Do not burn!

Prepare dipping sauces:
    Soy sauce dip:
        1/4 C soy sauce
        1 green onion, chopped
        coriander leaves (optional)
        1 Tables. garlic oil

    Catsup dip:
        1/4 C catsup
        1 Tables. Worcestershire sauce
        1 Tables. garlic oil

    Lemon juice dip:
        1/4 C lemon juice
        1 knob ginger root size of walnut, grated
        1 teas. salt
        1 Tables. garlic oil

Method:
    Put electric fry pan in center of table and bring chicken
broth to a boil with 4 slices of ginger root. Add water to
within 1/2 inch from top of pan.

    Divide and arrange raw food and dipping sauces around
table within easy reach of each diner. When broth boils, you
can start cooking. Use slotted spoons for cooking food. You
may provide one spoon per person or let one couple share one.
Cook as you eat. Do not overcook anything! Beef should be
pink in the middle; prawns turn from gray to white; chicken
turns white; bean cake warms through; oysters cook in 3 to 5
minutes; clams open up; Nappa cabbage and spinach may cook
until limp. Try different sauces with different foods. Replenish
broth or boiling water as broth evaporates.

The variety of foods you can cook is endless; i.e., roast pig (from Chinatown markets), fish fillets (bass), calves liver, squid, Chinese mustard greens, etc.

This is a different and fun way to entertain, somewhat like a fondue dinner, except that foods are cooked in chicken broth instead of oil. A 12-inch electric fry pan is convenient and hot enough to keep the broth boiling for 4 persons. For 6 to 8 persons, a larger pan with deeper sides (3 inches) is recommended. A stew pot is better than a shallow fry pan, especially for 6 to 8 persons. A fondue pot is not hot enough to cook for 4.

You can buy a special "Mongolian" pot designed for this. It is shaped like a large angel food cake pan. Charcoal is burned to heat the broth. A chimney lets out the fumes. Be sure to have plenty of ventilation and a pan of water under the pot to prevent burning your table top. These pots have no advantage over electric fry pans except that they are conversation pieces.

Instead of American-type slotted spoons, you can buy in oriental shops exotic little baskets with long handles. Chinese use bamboo chopsticks to hold on to the morsel of food while cooking. This prevents forgetting and overcooking the food.

APRICOT SAUCE

Substitute for plum sauce or chutney.
Soak together 20 minutes or more:
    8 oz. dried apricots
    1 3/4 C warm water
    1/4 C vinegar
    1/4 C granulated sugar
    1 clove garlic, smashed
    1/4 C grated ginger root
    2 Mexican dried red chilies; crumble
    dash salt
Put in a blender to chop for 5 minutes. Put in saucepan; cover and cook on lowest heat for 1/2 hour, stirring 2 to 3 times to prevent scorching. Add more water if necessary. Freeze or pour into sterilized jars and seal. Makes 3 half-pints.

If fresh apricots are used: Omit water to soak. Wash, quarter and pit 2 pounds apricots. Chop in blender with other ingredients. Add 4 pits to saucepan and simmer. Remove pits before jarring.

WATER CHESTNUT APPETIZERS

    1 can water chestnuts (5 oz.) drained
Marinate 20 minutes in:
    1 Tables. brown sugar
    1 Tables. soy sauce

    1 can pineapple tidbits

    8 slices bacon (approximately), cut in half the best way
        to distribute fat
Wrap 1 piece bacon around one water chestnut and one pineapple tidbit; secure with toothpick. Bake on rack at 375° - 400° for 20 minutes or until browned; drain on paper towels. Makes about 16 appetizers. To rewarm: put in 200° oven for 5 minutes.

A thin slice of chicken liver may be wrapped around the water chestnut and pineapple tidbit, then the bacon. Marinate liver slices with the water chestnuts.

SAUTÉED NAPPA CABBAGE (Chinese Cabbage)

The simplest way to cook a Chinese vegetable is to sauté it with oil, salt, ginger slices and/or smashed garlic.

1 1/2 pounds Nappa cabbage (p. 42),
    cut in half lengthwise (remove
    core); cut across stalk into 1-
    inch widths; wash
3 to 4 slices ginger root

Heat fry pan to high with 2 to 3 Tables. oil and ginger slices. Add cabbage and stir around; lower heat to prevent scorching, if necessary; cover to steam 2 or 3 minutes or until translucent. Remove ginger slices; drain cabbage before serving. May be held over.

A favorite among the Chinese is sautéed bok choy hearts, available in foodstores in Chinese communities. If you can't buy hearts, pick smaller stalks with lighter green leaves.

SWEET AND SOUR CABBAGE

1 American cabbage — 1 1/2 lbs. shredded 2 inches long
1 bell pepper, shredded 2 inches long
2 Tables. vinegar, any kind
2 Tables. white sugar

1/4 C pimiento, shredded

Sauté and salt cabbage and peppers with 2 Tables. oil one minute; add vinegar and sugar; cover and steam till translucent, adding water if necessary to prevent scorching. Toss in pimiento. May be held over.

JAI (rhymes with "eye")

3 slices ginger root
1/4 C oil
1 pound Nappa cabbage, washed and cut across length
   into 1-inch widths
1/2 pound winter melon, peeled and
   diced into 1-inch cubes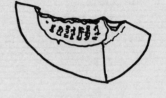
1 package of 3 age (pronounced
   "ah-gay" — Japanese name for
   deep-fried bean curd); cut up
   into 1-1/2-inch cubes
4 oz. bean threads — soften in warm water and cut
   into 4-inch lengths
1 can (5 oz.) bamboo shoots
1 oz. oriental mushrooms, reconstituted and sliced
1 can (11 oz.) chicken broth, regular strength

In a stew pot, on high heat, put in ginger root and oil. Add all the other ingredients; salt lightly; lower heat and simmer until winter melon is translucent. Add more water if necessary to prevent drying out. Add 2 Tables. oyster-flavored sauce; taste for salt before serving. Good warmed over. Instead of oyster sauce, Chinese use fermented bean cake (1 to 2 cubes), which has a pungent taste.

Jai is monks' food (meatless). It is also eaten by other Chinese especially during the first day of Chinese New Year in observance of a day of fast.

HOMEMADE NOODLES

   2 C flour
   2 teas. salt
Sift into a bowl. Make a well; add:
   2 eggs

   Starting at center, in a circular motion; mix with wooden
spoon to blend. Add:
   1/4 to 1/2 C cold water, a little at a time, until a
      ball forms.

   Knead on a floured board or countertop for 10 minutes,
using as much flour as necessary to prevent sticking to hands.
Cut into 4 portions; return to bowl; cover and rest 10 minutes.
Roll out each portion paper thin, rectangular shape, using as
much flour as necessary. Sift flour over top and bottom; roll
up like a loose jellyroll; cut across into thin strips with
cleaver. Spread out to dry 2 hours. Keeps 3 to 4 days in
refrigerator. Makes about 1 1/4 pounds.

For egg roll wrappers:
   Roll out as thin as you can. Makes about 12 wrappers.

牛肉

羊肉

BEEF AND LAMB

CURRIED BEEF TURNOVERS

Dough:
    2 C sifted all–purpose flour
    1/2 teas. salt
    3/4 C shortening
    about 1/3 C ice water

Mix flour and salt, cut shortening with flour. Add water a little at a time, using only enough to bind; form a ball and refrigerate 1/2 hour.

Meanwhile, make filling:
    3/4 lb. ground round
    1/2 round yellow onion, diced
    1 small clove garlic, minced
    1 Tables. dry sherry
    1 Tables. curry powder
    1 Tables. soy sauce
    salt to taste

    1 beaten egg

Sauté and break up ground round with onions and garlic and 2 Tables. oil till brown. Salt and add sherry, curry powder, and soy sauce and sauté once around; cool before filling dough.

Using a minimum of flour, roll out dough about 1/8 inch thick; cut rounds about 4 inches in diameter (use rim of coffee cup or pyrex dessert dish). Combine scraps and roll out again, using as little flour as necessary. Fill and fold in half; press edges together with fork. Moisten edges if necessary for a good seal; press with tines of fork to decorate. Place in a baking pan; brush top side with beaten egg. Bake in preheated oven at 425° for about 10 minutes. Tastes better hot. Can be rewarmed: Cover with foil and heat in 300° oven for 10 minutes.

Use your favorite piecrust recipe, if preferred.

BROCCOLI BEEF

1 flank steak, about 1 1/4 pounds, sliced

Mix with:

  1 Tables. cornstarch
  1 Tables. soy sauce
  1 clove garlic, minced or smashed
  3 to 4 slices ginger root
  salt to taste
  2 Tables. oil

Have ready:
  4 C fresh broccoli; cut flowerettes to get 1-inch heads
    and 1-inch stems. Strip leaves and outer fibers from
    stalks and discard. Cut stalks diagonally at a 45°
    angle 1/4 inch thick and 1 1/2 inches long. If
    stalks are more than 1 inch in diameter, cut in half
    lengthwise first before cutting diagonally.

Gravy ingredients, mix together:

  1 Tables. cornstarch
  1 Tables. soy sauce
  1 to 2 Tables. oyster-flavored sauce
  1/2 C water

Salt and sauté broccoli with about 3 Tables. oil over
high heat for about 1 minute. Add 2 to 3 Tables. water and
cover to steam till barely tender — takes less than 5 minutes.
Lower heat and stir if necessary to prevent scorching; remove
from pan.

Sauté meat in 2 separate batches on red hot heat with 2
Tables. oil until meat is browned on the outside and pink in
the middle. Add mixed gravy ingredients, scraping bottom of
pan; let gravy bubble once around. Return first batch of beef
and broccoli; toss to blend.

Variations: Substitute asparagus, zucchini, green beans, bok
choy, or cauliflower for broccoli, or use a combination of any of
these: Chinese pea pods, water chestnuts, bamboo shoots, mushrooms, celery, onions. Do try Broccoli Beef Chow Fun (p. 104).

This recipe turns out to be a great favorite, despite the hesitancy at first over oyster-flavored sauce and lukewarm enthusiasm for broccoli. A student of mine was quite a character when it came to the pleasures of the palate. Her husband did not care for broccoli, but she was determined he should not shortchange his taste buds. So she ate the flowerettes for lunch and saved the stalks for broccoli beef. She cut them on the diagonal and told him they were an "exotic Chinese vegetable" and he licked the platter clean!

I'm not suggesting that you practice such drastic means at deception, but don't let skepticism undermine your adventuresome spirit.

TO SLICE FLANK STEAK

Remove excess fat and membrane (if left on).

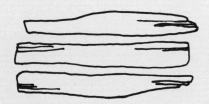

Cut steak into 2 or 3 strips so each is 2 to 2 1/2 inches wide.

Cut each strip across grain less than 1/4 inch thick, slanting cutting edge from fingers holding meat.

TOMATO BEEF AND PAN-FRIED NOODLES

Pan-Fried Noodles:
    1 pound fresh noodles

Bring to a brisk boil 3 quarts of water with 1 teas. salt and 1 Tables. oil in a 4-quart pot — deep enough to immerse a deep-fry basket. Loosen noodles so there are no clumps. Put about 1/2 pound noodles at a time into the basket; scald about 20 seconds, stirring all the while to prevent sticking together. Put basket under warm running water to wash off excess starch. Preheat fry pan with 2 Tables. oil; all at once spread noodles over entire bottom of pan; lightly brown one side on as high heat as possible without scorching (slow cooking dries out the noodles and causes them to be wiry); turn and brown the other side, adding more oil. To facilitate serving, pull apart the noodles with fingers into 6 or 8 sections. Transfer to platter; cover and keep warm in oven while you make Tomato Beef. Important: Do not scald noodles until fry pan is heated. Noodles gum together on standing. If they do, separate them by washing under warm tap water. Add 1 Tables. oil and toss with chopsticks.

Tomato Beef:
    1 flank steak, about 1 1/4 pound, sliced

Mix with:
    1 Tables. cornstarch
    1 Tables. soy sauce
    1 clove garlic, smashed
    3 to 4 slices ginger root, size of quarters
    salt to taste
    2 Tables. oil
Cut up into bite-size pieces the following:
    1 stalk tender celery
    1 medium yellow onion
    1 medium bell pepper
    3 medium tomatoes — remove skin by immersing in
        boiling water for 1/2 minute; cut into sixths
        or eighths. Whole canned tomatoes (1-pound

size) may be substituted; cut tomatoes in half;
save juice for gravy and use instead of water

Gravy ingredients, mix together:
  1 Tables. cornstarch
  1 Tables. soy sauce
  1 Tables. Worcestershire sauce
  2 Tables. catsup
  1 teas. sugar
  1 teas. curry powder
  1/2 C water or juice from canned tomatoes, if used

Salt as you sauté. Sauté celery, onions, and peppers
over medium-high heat for 1 minute; add tomatoes and sauté
another 1/2 minute (for canned tomatoes, just warm through);
remove from pan.

Wipe pan clean. Divide beef in 2 batches and sear each
in red hot heat until meat is browned on outside and pink in
the middle, using enough oil to prevent sticking. Add mixed
gravy ingredients, scraping the bottom of pan and stirring
until gravy bubbles once around. Return vegetables and toss
lightly to blend.

Serve mixed with noodles or over them, or serve with
rice.

Noodles may be fried days ahead and refrigerated. To
rewarm: Sprinkle water over; cover with foil; rewarm in 300°
oven 20 minutes.

OYSTER SAUCE BEEF AND SOYBEAN CAKE SAUTÉ

1 flank steak—1 1/4 pounds or more, sliced (p. 85)

Mix with:
    1 Tables. cornstarch
    1 Tables. soy sauce
    3 to 4 slices ginger root
    salt to taste
    2 Tables. oil

1 soybean cake (4 x 5-inch block), drain in colander
    an hour ahead. Cut into 1-inch cubes; drain
    thoroughly dry on paper towels; change towels
    as they get wet.

1/2 pound fresh Chinese pea pods, string first; cut
    large ones diagonally in half to match small ones
    the size of your little finger.

Gravy ingredients, mix together:
    1/2 C water or broth
    1 Tables. cornstarch
    1 Tables. soy sauce
    2 Tables. oyster-flavored sauce

Heat 3 Tables. oil in fry pan on low heat for 5 minutes.
Turn heat up till pan is hot; add soybean cake and lightly
brown; turn with spatula and brown one other side, adding
more oil when necessary; salt; transfer to platter.

Salt and sauté Chinese pea pods with 2 Tables. oil for
1/2 minute; add to soybean cake.

Sear meat in 2 separate batches with 2 Tables. oil each
till brown outside and pink in the middle. Add mixed gravy
ingredients; stir till thickened, scraping bottom of pan.
Return bean cake and pea pods; gently toss with chopsticks
to mix.

BEEF AND CHINESE PEA PODS OVER SNOW

    1 flank steak, about 1 1/4 pounds, sliced (p. 85)
Mix with:
    1 Tables. cornstarch
    1 Tables. soy sauce
    1 clove garlic, smashed or minced
    3 slices ginger root
    2 Tables. oil
    salt to taste

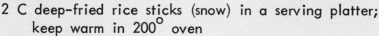

Have ready:
    2 teas. hoisin sauce
    2 C deep-fried rice sticks (snow) in a serving platter;
        keep warm in 200° oven
    1/4 pound Chinese pea pods, leave whole for
        small ones the size of your little finger, or
        cut diagonally in half for large ones
Gravy ingredients, mix together:
    1 Tables. cornstarch
    1 Tables. soy sauce
    2 teas. sugar
    5/8 C chicken broth (1/2 C + 2 Tables.)

    Sauté pea pods over medium-high heat with 1 Tables. oil
for about 1 minute; remove from pan.
    Divide beef into 2 batches and sauté each batch over red
hot heat with 2 Tables. oil until beef is browned outside and
pink in the middle. Return first batch of beef; add hoisin sauce;
sauté once around; add mixed gravy ingredients, scraping bottom
of pan; spread over rice sticks. Spread pea pods over top.
    Variation: To substitute for rice sticks, use instant or
deep-fried noodles.

GINGER BEEF
    Use above recipe; omit sugar and hoisin sauce; double
ginger slices; top with slivered green onions.

PEPPERED STEAK
    Slivered green peppers, 2 inches long, may be substituted
for snow peas.

MONGOLIAN LAMB

2 C lean lamb (leg or chops), about 1 1/2 lbs., sliced
thinly into pieces 1 by 2 inches

Mix with:
1 Tables. cornstarch
1 Tables. soy sauce
2 Tables. oil
4 drops liquid smoke (Wright's Bar-B-Q or other)
1/2 teas. Tabasco sauce or hot chili sauce
1 large clove garlic, smashed or minced
3 to 4 slices ginger root
salt and pepper to taste

Have ready:
2 Tables. or more sherry
1 Tables. hoisin sauce

1 yellow onion cut bite size
1/4 pound Chinese pea pods — cut large ones diagonally
in half; leave ones the size of your small finger
whole

Gravy ingredients; mix together:
1 Tables. cornstarch
1 Tables. Worcestershire sauce
few drops Tabasco or hot chili sauce
5/8 C chicken broth (1/2 C + 2 Tables.)

Salt and sauté onions with 2 Tables. oil over high heat
for 1 minute; add Chinese pea pods; salt and sauté another
1/2 minute; remove from pan. Sauté lamb in 2 separate
batches over high heat with 2 Tables. oil till browned and
barely done — takes less than 5 minutes. Return first batch of
meat; sizzle in sherry and hoisin sauce. Add gravy ingredients, scraping bottom of pan. Return vegetables and toss
lightly to blend.

Variation: 1 C frozen green peas or 1 bell pepper, cut
bite size, may be substituted for Chinese pea pods. Sauté
along with onions.

LAMB AND VEGETABLES

Cutting pattern: sliver meat and vegetables like cocktail picks.

    2 C lean lamb (chops or leg), about 1 1/2 lbs.

Mix with:
    1 Tables. cornstarch
    1 Tables. soy sauce
    2 Tables. oil
    4 slices ginger root
    1 large clove garlic, smashed
    salt to taste

    2 Tables. sherry

    1/2 C oriental mushrooms, reconstituted first
    1 C bamboo shoots
    1 C tender celery
    1/2 yellow onion
    1 C fresh Chinese pea pods, string first

Have ready:
    2 C deep-fried rice sticks, crumbled (p. 44)

Gravy ingredients, mix together:
    1 Tables. cornstarch
    1 Tables. soy sauce
    5/8 C water from mushrooms

Salt as needed. Divide meat into 2 batches and sear separately in fry pan with 2 Tables. oil each until lamb is brown outside and pink in the middle; sizzle in sherry; remove from pan. Sauté mushrooms and bamboo shoots 1 minute with 3 Tables. oil; add 2 Tables. water; cover to steam for 2 minutes. Add celery, onions and pea pods and sauté 1 minute. Return meat to pan; add mixed gravy ingredients and toss lightly till thickened. Top with rice sticks.

Variation: Substitute chicken or beef.

BARBECUED LAMB

1 leg of lamb, 6 lbs., boned and skinned. Leave some
     fat on. Cut into 1-inch cubes.

Marinate with:
    1/4 C soy sauce
    1/4 C sherry
    1/4 C catsup
    1/4 C oil
    1/4 C water
    2 Tables. Worcestershire sauce
    1 Tables. curry powder
    few drops Tabasco sauce
    2 cloves garlic, smashed
    6 slices peeled ginger root, size of quarters
    1/4 C fresh coriander, chopped (optional)
    1 whole yellow onion, chopped
    salt and pepper

Let stand 8 hours. Put on skewers with 1/4 inch space
between. Lay on grill when charcoal turns white. Brush
marinade over and turn meat as necessary to prevent burning.
Lamb may be eaten pink in the middle. Serve American-
style.

Variation: Instead of curry, use 1/2 teas. Chinese five-
spices powder.

Serves 8.

猪肉

PORK

BARBECUED PORK (CHA SIEW — rhymes with "view")

Cut into 3/4-inch thick steaks:
   3 to 4 pounds pork loin, butt, shoulder or tenderloin

Marinate with:
   2 Tables. brown sugar or honey
   2 Tables. soy sauce
   2 Tables. pale dry sherry
   salt to taste
   1 Tables. hoisin sauce (optional)
   1/2 teas. saltpeter — turns the
      meat pink (optional)
   pinch of five-fragrant-spices
      (optional)

Let stand 8 hours or overnight, turning once. Bake on a rack in a broiler pan in a 500° oven 15 to 20 minutes on each side or until done and browned. Save marinade and add 5 minutes before pork is done. If further browning is needed, heat may be turned up the last 5 minutes.

   Hint: Make extra batches for your freezer. Great shredded for egg foo young and egg rolls, garnish for wun tun soup and pork chop suey chow mein, and sliced up for hors d'oeuvres and sandwiches.

BARBECUED SPARERIBS (SIEW PIE GWUT)

   Buy a whole sparerib, about 2 1/2 pounds. Small spareribs come from younger animals and the flavor is more delicate. Marinate with the same ingredients as for barbecued pork.

   Bake whole the same amount of time. Five minutes before removing from oven, brush on a glaze of 1/4 C brown sugar or honey and 1/4 C boiling water (variation: substitute for water, heated orange juice concentrate or pineapple juice concentrate). Cut between the ribs and serve whole (finger food) or cut ribs into 1-1/2-inch pieces (when using chopsticks).

   A great favorite among Chinese for large buffet parties; it can be made ahead of time (frozen, too) and warmed up in batches in foil as party progresses.

SWEET AND SOUR PORK

2 to 3 C boned, lean pork (about 1 1/2 pounds) —
    butt or loin, cut into 1-inch cubes

Season with:
    1 Tables. dry sherry
    1 Tables. soy sauce
    1 clove garlic, minced or smashed
    1 Tables. or less ginger root, grated or smashed
    salt to taste

Stand at least 20 minutes. Mix in 1/4 C flour and then press each cube with more flour.

Cut up the following vegetables into bite-size pieces (pp. 12-14):
    1 small bell pepper
    1 small yellow onion
    1 carrot, parboil first till fork-tender (select slender
        carrots for tenderness)
    1 tomato, remove skin (steam 1/2 minute in pot when
        parboiling carrot)

    1 can (1 pound 4 oz.) pineapple chunks — save juice
        for gravy

Gravy ingredients, mix together:
    1 1/2 Tables. cornstarch
    1 Tables. soy sauce
    2 Tables. sugar (brown or white)
    2 Tables. vinegar
    2 Tables. catsup
    3/4 C pineapple juice
    few drops of red food coloring (optional)

Heat fry pan till red hot with 3 Tables. oil. Lay pork cubes one by one in a single layer without crowding or agitating. Brown meat on one side till crust forms. Turn meat and brown other side without agitating, adding more oil if necessary. Lower heat to finish cooking pork — about 5 more minutes, covering partially. Remove from pan. Clean fry pan if necessary.

Salt and sauté peppers and onions on medium-high heat with 2 Tables. oil for 1 minute; add tomatoes and sauté 1/2 minute; add carrots, pineapples and mixed gravy ingredients, stirring only until gravy bubbles once around and turns translucent. Toss in meat.

Variations: Substitute spareribs cut into 1-1/2-inch lengths, or use chicken or prawns.

To make ahead: Fry meat and refrigerate or freeze. The day of serving: Thaw to room temperature; rewarm in 300° oven in shallow casserole 20 to 30 minutes. Sauté vegetables briefly and make gravy; toss with pork cubes as close to serving time as is comfortable for you.

Deep-fried method:

Follow same procedure and let pork cubes stand in seasonings at least 20 minutes. At this point the procedure changes. Make a batter with 2 Tables. cornstarch, 2 Tables. Bisquick and 2 Tables. water. Add pork cubes and coat; then roll each pork cube with bread crumbs or cracker meal. Deep-fry in 2 inches of oil 375° for 5 minutes or more until done — cut open to check. Drain on paper towels. Follow recipe through for vegetables and gravy.

Fry pork cubes ahead and refrigerate or freeze.

PORK CHOP SUEY CHOW MEIN

Cutting pattern for meat and vegetables: shreds to match bean sprouts.

Chop suey means a little bit of this and that (meat, celery, bean sprouts, etc.). Chow mein means fried noodles.

1 pound fresh noodles — pan-fry as for Tomato Beef
(p. 86) or brown 8 inches under the broiler
with oven door shut

Scald noodles the same as for Tomato Beef, but instead of browning in fry pan, put noodles in a 9-inch by 13-inch cake pan; add 2 Tables. or more oil and 1 Tables. soy sauce and mix. Spread evenly and put under the broiler 5 minutes on each side to brown, watching carefully to prevent scorching. You can scald 1 pound of noodles at a time if you have at least 4 quarts of boiling water. This method uses less oil and saves time when cooking large quantities. Pull apart noodles to facilitate serving.

Pork Chop Suey:
2 C pork (loin or butt)
1 clove garlic, smashed

2 Tables. dry sherry

1/2 C bamboo shoots
3/4 C oriental mushrooms, reconstituted;
discard stems; save water for gravy

1/2 C onions
1/2 C celery

1/4 pound Chinese pea pods, string as for
string beans first
1/4 pound bean sprouts

Gravy ingredients, mix together:
    1 Tables. cornstarch
    1 Tables. soy sauce
    3/4 C water from soaking mushrooms
    dash MSG

Garnish:
    2 stalks green onions
    1/4 C fresh whole coriander leaves (optional)
    1/2 C barbecued pork (optional)

Salt as needed. In red hot fry pan sauté pork with 2 Tables. oil and garlic until pork is browned and done — takes a few minutes to dry out juice. Sizzle in sherry; remove from pan. Sauté bamboo shoots and mushrooms with 2 Tables. oil for one minute; add 2 Tables. water; cover and steam 2 minutes. Add onions and celery and sauté another minute; add to pork. Sauté pea pods and bean sprouts with 2 Tables. oil for 1 minute; return pork and vegetables to pan; add mixed gravy ingredients; toss lightly with chopsticks till gravy thickens. Spread over or mix in with noodles.

Garnish with green onions, coriander leaves and barbecued pork. At the table serve with mustard paste (p. 42), Chinese red vinegar (p. 47), and sesame oil.

Variations: Substitute chicken, prawns, ham in any combination or combined with pork. If meat is already cooked, just add to warm through.

Noodles may be made days ahead; cover and refrigerate. To rewarm: sprinkle with water; cover with foil; rewarm in 300° oven 20 minutes.

SESAME SEED PORK CUBES

   3 C pork cubes with 1-inch sides

Mix with:
   1 Tables. soy sauce
   1 Tables. sherry
   1 Tables. ginger root, smashed or grated
   1 Tables. coriander, minced (optional)
   1 clove garlic, smashed
   salt to taste

Stand 20 minutes.

Batter, mix together:
   3 Tables. cornstarch
   3 Tables. Bisquick
   3 Tables. cold water

   Add to pork cubes and mix. Roll and press pork cubes firmly with sesame seeds. Deep-fry at 375° in 2 inches of oil for about 5 minutes or until done. Cut open to check. Drain on paper towels. Can be made ahead and rewarmed in oven—300° for 10 to 15 minutes. Serve with cocktail picks.

   Variations: Use chicken instead of pork; finely chopped walnuts or peanuts instead of sesame seeds.

BARBECUED PORK AND CUCUMBER SALAD

1 cucumber, peel and cut in half lengthwise,
   remove seeds

Lay flat side down and cut diagonally 1/8 inch thick.
Taste cucumber; if bitter, cover with water; add 1 teas. salt;
stand 5 minutes; rinse and drain.

Marinate at least 10 minutes with:
   4 Tables. vinegar
   5 Tables. sugar

Drain after 10 minutes.

1 C barbecued pork, ham or chicken, sliver

2 C deep-fried rice sticks, crumble

2 Tables. sesame seeds, toast with 1 teas. sesame oil
   in fry pan; stir, do not scorch!

2 green onions, sliver

Toss all together just before serving.

FUN

Fun is a cooked dough made from rice and water and then steamed. It is available in foodstores in Chinatown. In the native method, rice is soaked in water to soften and stone-ground with water added. Today we can substitute a blender, saving much time and labor.

1 C long-grain rice; wash and add cold water 1 inch above the level of rice. Refrigerate and soak about 48 hours. Add cold water to rice to make up to 2 C; add 1 teas. salt and 1 Tables. oil. Put in blender for 5 minutes or more to liquefy. Now batter is ready for steaming to make fun.

Set up steamer and have water bubbling. Have two 8-inch round cake pans ready; add 1 teas. oil to each to coat bottom. Pour 1/4 C batter in each pan to coat evenly; put one pan in steamer. Cover and steam 2 minutes; take a peek and, if necessary, tip pan to fill in low spots. Continue to steam another 3 minutes or more until fun is translucent and large bubbles form. Remove from steamer; cool about 5 minutes. Put second pan in steamer and continue in same manner, adding 1 teas. oil to each pan thereafter. (Replenish water in steamer as needed.) When the fun in first pan has cooled, roll up like a jellyroll right in the pan. Transfer to a platter; can be piled on each other.

Makes 8 rolls.

If 9-inch cake pans are used, increase batter by 2 Tables. to each pan — makes 5 rolls.

Fun can be made ahead and refrigerated; cover with plastic wrap; keeps 4 to 5 days.

Fun can be frozen; freezer wrap; takes 8 hours to thaw.

102

FUN — SHORT-CUT METHOD

Put into a bowl:
> 2 C unsifted Swansdown cake flour; pack down by hitting
>   bottom of measuring cup against countertop.
> 3 Tables. cornstarch
> 2 teas. salt
> 3 Tables. vegetable oil

Add slowly and beat on medium speed until smooth:
> 2 1/2 C cold water

If lumps form, strain through fine-gauge sieve. Steam as in preceding recipe.

BARBECUED PORK AND BEAN SPROUTS CHOW FUN

> 1 recipe fun (preceding page) — 8 rolls, cut each roll
>   into 1-inch widths. If fun has been refrigerated
>   or frozen, thaw first

Heat fry pan or dutch oven with 2 Tables. oil; add fun and 2 Tables. water; cover. Lower heat and warm through — about 5 to 10 minutes. You can also warm fun in a bowl by steaming 5 to 10 minutes.

Meanwhile:
Beat and salt 2 eggs. Heat fry pan with oil to coat the bottom of pan. Add eggs to cover entire pan; golden brown both sides. Roll up like jellyroll and transfer to chopping board. When cool, cut into thin strips across; add to fun.

Heat fry pan till red hot with 4 Tables. oil. Add:

> 2 C. barbecued pork, shredded
> 1/2 pound bean sprouts
> 1/4 pound Chinese pea pods, cut to match
>   bean sprouts
> 1 teas. sugar
> salt
> dash MSG

Sauté 1 to 2 minutes; drain off liquid; add to fun.

Add:
  1 Tables. soy sauce
  1/2 teas. sesame oil
  1 Tables. oyster sauce (optional)

Use chopsticks to toss together like a salad.

BROCCOLI BEEF CHOW FUN

Make Broccoli Beef (p. 84) and one recipe fun.

Heat up fun as in preceding recipe. Toss the two together and you have a sumptuous feast in one dish.

STEAMED SPARERIBS

  1 1/4 pounds lean riblets, have butcher cut them
      1 1/2 inches long

Mix with the following in a 1-quart heatproof bowl:
  1 Tables. cornstarch
  1 Tables. soy sauce
  1 Tables. sherry
  1 Tables. hoisin sauce
  2 Tables. lemon juice
  1/4 lemon peel, washed and sliced
  salt to taste
  1 clove garlic, smashed
  3 to 4 slices ginger root
  salt to taste
  dash MSG

Spread evenly in bowl and steam 1/2 hour or more, turning once after 15 minutes. Remove lemon peel, ginger slices and extra fat before serving. Delicious with rice.

Excellent reheated.

PORK, GREEN BEANS AND MUSHROOM SAUTÉ

Cutting pattern: all vegetables are diced 1/4-inch cubes.

1 pound lean ground pork
1 clove garlic, smashed or minced

2 Tables. pale dry sherry

1 pkg. frozen green beans, thawed, or 1/2 pound
    fresh green beans, or Chinese long beans
1/4 C oriental mushrooms, reconstituted in 1/4 C
    warm water or 1/2 C fresh mushrooms
1/2 C jicama, peeled, or 1 can (5 oz.)
    water chestnuts

Gravy ingredients, mix together:
    1 C chicken broth
    1 Tables. soy sauce
    1 Tables. cornstarch

1/4 to 1/2 C chopped cocktail peanuts

Salt as needed. In red hot fry pan sauté pork with garlic till browned and done – takes a few minutes to dry out the juice; remove excess oil; sizzle in sherry; sauté once around; transfer to dish.

Sauté green beans, oriental mushrooms and jicama with 4 Tables. oil for 2 minutes. Add water if necessary; cover to steam between stirrings. If fresh green beans or Chinese long beans are used, add 1/4 C water and cover to cook. If fresh mushrooms are used, add about 1/2 minute before beans are tender.

Return pork to pan; add mixed gravy ingredients; stir till thickened. Sprinkle peanuts over.

If fresh water chestnuts are available, they make the dish.

Variation: Add 1 Tables. hoisin sauce or oyster sauce to gravy ingredients.

Give this dish a flair by serving with lettuce cups. Wash and drain lettuce; tear lettuce the size of your palm; spoon pork mixture in lettuce; fold over like a taco and eat with fingers — good also as an hors d'oeuvre.

PORK AND PRAWNS STUFFED PEPPERS

Filling, cut up first and then mince together:
    1/2 pound prawns, shelled and deveined
    1/2 pound pork, any cut
    1 whole green onion

Put into a bowl and mix in:
    1 Tables. cornstarch
    1 Tables. soy sauce
    1/2 teas. sesame oil
    dash MSG
    salt and pepper

    3 medium bell peppers, cut in half crosswise and then
        each half in quarters. Remove seeds but leave in
        some of the white membranes which help hold in
        filling. Trim stem.

    2 Tables. sherry

Sauce:
    1 small clove garlic minced like paste with:
    2 teas. salted black beans — wash through strainer first

    1 Tables. soy sauce
    1 teas. cornstarch
    1/2 C chicken broth

Stuff each piece of bell pepper fully, firmly and smoothly. Heat fry pan to medium high with 4 Tables. oil. Lay peppers meat side down and fry till golden brown; turn to brown one other side. Sizzle in 2 Tables. sherry; lower heat; cover and cook till done — takes about 5 minutes. Transfer to serving dish with filling side up, arranging them neatly.

Clean fry pan if necessary. Sauté black beans and garlic with 1 Tables. oil for 1/2 minute on high heat; add remaining sauce ingredients which have been mixed together; stir till translucent. Pour over peppers.

May be made ahead and rewarmed in oven, covered.

Variations: Stuff large fresh Chinese pea pods. For zesty hot dish: stuff chili peppers. For Chinese only: stuff bitter melon.

STEAMED PORK WITH DRIED FISH (HOM YUE)

(I slipped in this recipe for my Japanese friends.)

Put in a shallow, heatproof bowl the following, mix and spread evenly:
> 2 C pork (loin or butt), thinly sliced or ground
> 1 Tables. cornstarch
> 1 Tables. soy sauce
> 1 Tables. sherry
> salt to taste
> dash MSG

Lay on top:
> 1 piece dried fish,* about 1 1/2 by 3 inches. Wash and remove scales and clean out entrails, if any

On top of fish, put:
> 1 piece dried tangerine peel, the size of your thumb. Soak in warm water 1/2 hour to soften first and then sliver
> 1 teas. ginger root, slivered
> 1 clove garlic, smashed

Steam for 1/2 hour or until done.
Suggestion: make lots of rice!
Good reheated.

*Dried salted fish is available in Chinatown foodstores, whole or cut up. Some are cut up and jarred in oil. Ask for "hom yue."

PORK AND SOYBEAN CURD

Cutting pattern: meat and vegetables shredded to match sprouts

> 1 bean cake (4 by 5 inches, blue label), drain in colander
> an hour ahead; cut into 1-inch cubes; drain some more
> on paper towels; keep changing towels until dry

> 1/4 pound bean sprouts, wash and drain
> 1/4 pound Chinese pea pods, string as for string beans
> first (leave whole if uniformly tiny — the size of
> your small finger)
> 1 stalk tender celery

> 2 C pork (butt or loin)
> 1 small clove garlic, smashed or minced

> 2 Tables. dry sherry
> 2 Tables. bean sauce (also known as soybean
> condiment), mashed

Gravy ingredients:
> 1 Tables. cornstarch
> 1 Tables. soy sauce
> 3/4 C chicken broth

Garnish: 2 stalks green onions

Salt as needed. To minimize sticking, warm fry pan on
low heat with 4 Tables. oil for 5 minutes. Turn heat to high
until pan is red hot. Place bean cake cubes gently into fry
pan side by side; lightly brown one side; turn and brown one
other side; remove from pan without breaking.

Over high heat with 2 Tables. oil, sauté bean sprouts,
pea pods and celery; add to bean cake.

Sauté pork with 2 Tables. oil and garlic over sizzling
heat until pork is done and brown — takes a few minutes to dry
out juice; remove extra fat, if necessary. Add mashed bean
sauce and sherry and sauté another 15 seconds. Mix in gravy
ingredients; stirring till thickened. Return vegetables, bean
cake and toss lightly to blend. Garnish with green onions.

The robust flavor of the bean sauce adds character to
the bean cake.

鸡
鸭

POULTRY

CURRIED CHICKEN

3 C boned, raw chicken, cut into chunks the size
   of your whole thumb. Season with salt and
   pepper; dredge in flour

In a stew pot with 3 Tables. oil over medium-high heat,
without agitating, brown chicken on one side; turn to brown
one other side, adding more oil if necessary.

Add:
   1 clove garlic, minced or smashed
   1 large knob ginger root, size of a walnut,
      peeled and sliced
   1 Tables. soy sauce
   1 Tables. Worcestershire sauce
   1 Tables. dry sherry
   1 Tables. sugar
   1 Tables. or more curry powder

Add the following which have been cut into bite-size pieces:
   1 yellow onion
   1 bell pepper
   1 stalk celery
   1 potato
Sauté once around.

Add 1 can (8 oz.) tomato sauce and 1 can water; salt.
Cover and simmer until potatoes are done, about 20 minutes.
Add more water if necessary to prevent burning. Serve with
rice. Excellent prepared ahead.

You can make this American-style. Use serving-size
pieces of chicken parts: legs, thighs or breasts (cut in half).

CORIANDER CHICKEN SALAD

Cutting pattern: shreds like toothpicks.

> 2 pounds chicken parts — breasts, legs or thighs, leave
>   skin on

Marinate in the following which have been mixed together:
> 2 Tables. soy sauce
> 2 Tables. sherry
> 2 Tables. vegetable oil
> 2 Tables. water
> 4 Tables. coriander leaves and/or stems, or 2
>   whole green onions, cut into 1-inch lengths
> 1 Tables. hoisin sauce
> 1 Tables. grated ginger root
> 1 teas. sesame oil
> 1 teas. dry mustard
> salt to taste

Stand at least 2 hours before baking — preferably overnight.

Place chicken on rack over foil-lined pan; reserve marinade. Bake in preheated oven 450°, 15 to 20 minutes on each
side or until browned and done. Switch over to "broil" for
about 1 minute if further browning is needed. For breasts, lay
skin side up; it is not necessary to turn unless skin is over-
browning. Pour the reserved marinade over chicken the last 2
minutes of baking to cook it. Cool and shred fine along the
grain. Use as much of the skin as preferred and shred with
cleaver. Skim off excess fat from drippings; mix in 1 Tables.
dry mustard right in the pan; add chicken and mop up all the
drippings. If drippings have dried out, add a few tablespoons
boiling water to dissolve.

Have ready:
> 1/2 C finely chopped cocktail peanuts (not Spanish
>   peanuts) or almonds
> 1/4 C sesame seeds browned with 1 teas. sesame oil
>   in fry pan; stir, do not scorch!
> 2 C deep-fried rice sticks (p. 44)

The 3 above ingredients may be combined.

112

The 3 ingredients below may be combined:
   2 C iceberg lettuce, shredded
   2 stalks green onions, shredded
   1/4 C fresh coriander leaves, leave whole — can be
      picked out for those who have not acquired a
      taste for it

When ready to serve, toss everything together very lightly with chopsticks. Sprinkle 2 Tables. Chinese red vinegar over. Serve extra vinegar and sesame oil at the table.

Deep-fry method:
   2 pounds chicken

Marinate as above. Press with cornstarch; spread out in heatproof bowl; steam 30 minutes or until done.

Transfer chicken to a clean bowl and refrigerate overnight, or place on a rack and air-dry 4 hours.

Deep-fry in 400° oil till golden. Cool; remove bones. Shred skin with cleaver; shred meat along grain with fingers. Add 1 Tables. mustard paste. Toss with ingredients as above (beginning with "Have ready:"). For richer flavor, add a few tablespoons oil from deep-frying chicken.

Everything can be done the day before. Do not refrigerate peanuts, sesame seeds and rice sticks. Toss salad together just before serving.

This marinade is excellent for barbecues and for roasting whole chickens — make more marinade.

FRIED CHICKEN WING DRUMSTICKS

1 pound or more meaty chicken wings, cut up as
   illustrated

Marinate 20 minutes in:
   1 Tables. soy sauce
   1 Tables. sherry
   1 small clove minced garlic
   3 or 4 slices ginger root the size of quarters
   salt to taste

Have ready:
   1 egg white, beaten slightly

   water chestnut powder (cornstarch or tapioca starch
      may be substituted) for coating chicken

Coat chicken thinly with egg white; press firmly on all
sides with water chestnut powder; spread out and air-dry for
20 minutes (to minimize spattering when deep-frying).

Heat 2 inches oil to 400°. Fry chicken without agitating
until done — takes 3 to 5 minutes. Cut open to check for doneness. Fry as many as there is space for as long as the temperature
is maintained. Serve with mustard paste (p. 42), Sweet and Sour
Sauce (p. 116), or Cocktail Sauce (p. 116).

TO SHAPE CHICKEN WING DRUMSTICKS

1. Cut off wing tip
   (discard) to reveal
   2 bones in lower wing.
   Disjoint lower and upper
   wing.

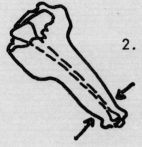

2. Upper wing has one bone. Cut and loosen tendons at smaller end; push meat up to the shoulder bone; invert meat like inside-out umbrella so . . .

3. . . . you have one drumstick.

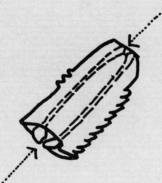

4. Lower wing has 2 bones. Cut tendons between 2 bones on both ends to separate (arrows). Cut tendons at smaller end of bones.

5. Remove the smaller bone with right hand, holding on firmly to meat with left hand.

6. Push meat up toward larger end; invert meat as for upper wing. Now you have a second drumstick.

SWEET AND SOUR SAUCE

In a saucepan, combine, cook and stir till thickened:
  - 6 to 8 maraschino cherries
  - 1 can (8 oz.) pineapple, cut into chunks
  - 1 1/2 Tables. cornstarch
  - 1 Tables. soy sauce
  - 1 Tables. vinegar
  - 1 Tables. sugar, brown or white (optional)
  - 2 Tables. catsup
  - 2 Tables. juice from maraschino cherries
  - 1/2 C juice from pineapple (make up with water
      if necessary)

COCKTAIL SAUCE

Mix together:
  - 1 C catsup
  - 1 Tables. Worcestershire sauce
  - 1 Tables. lemon juice
  - 1 Tables. chopped onion or 1 teas. onion flakes

ASPARAGUS CHICKEN WITH BLACK BEAN SAUCE

  - 2 C boned raw chicken (1 1/2 lbs.), cut up into
      pieces the size of your whole thumb; remove
      excess skin

Mix with:
  - 1 Tables. cornstarch
  - 1 Tables. soy sauce
  - 1 Tables. Chinese salted black beans; wash through
      a strainer and mince like paste with:
  - 2 large cloves garlic

  - 2 Tables. oil
  - salt to taste

4 C fresh asparagus spears, snap off and discard
    tough, whitish ends; slice spears diagonally,
    as shown, 1/4 inch thick and 1 1/2 inches
    long. Asparagus as big around as your thumb
    is the best size. Big ones have too much white
    parts to discard. Skinny ones do not look as
    pretty.

Gravy ingredients, mix together:
    1 Tables. cornstarch
    1 Tables. soy sauce
    1 teas. sugar
    dash MSG
    5/8 C broth (1/2 C + 2 Tables.)

Sauté and salt asparagus in fry pan with 2 Tables. oil
over high heat for 1 minute; cover and steam another 1/2
minute, adding 1 Tables. of water if necessary to prevent
scorching; remove from pan.

Sear chicken with 2 Tables. oil over high heat until
done — takes about 5 minutes. Add mixed gravy ingredients
and stir until thickened, scraping bottom of pan. Return
asparagus to pan; toss lightly together.

Variations: Substitute beef for chicken; cauliflower or
zucchini for asparagus.

In preparing ahead, remember asparagus waters excessively. It is best to sauté the last minute and toss in.

CASHEW CHICKEN

3 C boned raw chicken (about 1 3/4 pounds breasts,
   legs or thighs), cut into pieces half the size
   of your whole thumb; discard excess skin

Mix with:
   1 Tables. cornstarch
   1 Tables. soy sauce
   1 Tables. dry sherry
   1 small clove garlic, smashed
   3 or 4 slices ginger root, the size of quarters
   2 Tables. oil
   salt to taste
Let stand 20 minutes before cooking.

Meanwhile, dice the following the size of cashews:
   about 1/2 C oriental mushrooms (soak 1/2 hr.
      in 1/2 C warm water to reconstitute); save
      water for gravy
   1/2 C yellow onions
   1/2 C bamboo shoots
   1/2 C tender celery
   1 small can button mushrooms (about 5 oz.), save
      juice for gravy
   1/4 pound Chinese pea pods; string as for string
      beans first. (If these are dainty, the size of
      your small finger, leave whole.)

Gravy ingredients:
   1 Tables. cornstarch
   1 Tables. soy sauce
   1 teas. sugar
   1/4 teas. MSG
   5/8 C water from both mushrooms
   few drops sesame oil

Have ready:
   1 C ready-to-eat cashews; warm in 200° oven
      5 minutes before serving

118

On high heat salt and sauté oriental mushrooms and bamboo shoots with 3 Tables. oil for 1 minute; add 2 to 3 Tables. water to prevent scorching; cover and steam 2 to 3 minutes. Add onions and celery; salt and sauté 1 minute; add pea pods and button mushrooms; salt and sauté 1 minute; remove all the vegetables from pan.

Sauté chicken over red hot heat with 2 Tables. oil until browned and done, scraping the bottom of pan to minimize sticking. Divide into 2 batches to sauté if necessary to prevent slow cooking and watering. Add mixed gravy ingredients, scraping bottom of pan and stirring lightly till thickened. Return vegetables and mix; garnish with cashews.

The same recipe can be used for almond, peanut or walnut chicken. If raw nuts are used, they are delicious deep-fried: heat oil to 375°; put nuts in a strainer and deep-fry till golden.

Other variations: Use bell peppers, green peas, water chestnuts, jicama, fresh mushrooms.

SESAME CHICKEN

2 C (1 1/2 lbs. legs, thighs, or breasts) boned, raw chicken without skin; cut into pieces the size of your whole thumb. Add and mix in order:

1 Tables. soy sauce	1 clove garlic, smashed or minced
1 Tables. dry sherry	3 to 4 slices peeled ginger root
1 Tables. oil	salt to taste
1/4 teas. MSG	1/4 C cornstarch

Roll each piece of chicken in sesame seeds. Spread out on platter for 20 minutes before frying.

1 pound asparagus (select ones as big around as your thumb). Snap off tough ends and discard. Cut asparagus diagonally 1/4 inch thick and 1 1/2 inches long.

White sauce ingredients. Put together in bowl:
1 1/4 C light cream (half-and-half)
1 Tables. cornstarch
1 Tables. chicken-flavored soup base (or 1 bouillon cube)
2 Tables. butter

Have ready:
1/4 C sesame seeds slightly browned by shaking or stirring in fry pan — do not scorch!

Heat 4 Tables. oil in a fry pan till hot. Lay chicken pieces one by one, single-layer and brown one side; turn and brown the opposite side. Cook till done — takes about 5 minutes total. Transfer to warmed platter.

Wipe pan clean; salt and sauté asparagus with 2 Tables. oil on medium-high heat for 1 to 2 minutes; drain off liquid. Surround chicken with it. (If held over, put asparagus aside in a dish first as it weeps on standing. Drain and then surround chicken just before serving.)

Wipe pan clean; add white sauce ingredients and stir till butter melts and cornstarch thickens. Pour over chicken and asparagus. Sprinkle browned sesame seeds over.

Variation: Substitute for asparagus: 1/4 lb. fresh Chinese pea pods or 1 pkg. (7 oz.) frozen green peas or 1/4 lb. broccoli.

CHICKEN WITH LICHEES AND PINEAPPLES

1 1/2 to 2 pounds chicken breasts with skin; split if whole

Season with:
1 Tables. soy sauce
1 Tables. sherry
few slices ginger root
salt to taste

Press firmly with cornstarch all around. Spread out in a heatproof bowl and steam 20 to 30 minutes or until done, turning once at midpoint. (Set the timer when water begins to boil; lower heat but keep water bubbling.) When chicken is done, lay on rack to air-dry for 1 hour or more before deep-frying.

Meanwhile, make gravy in saucepan:
1 Tables. cornstarch
1 Tables. soy sauce
1 Tables. catsup
dash MSG
3/4 C pineapple and lichee juice

Stir till it bubbles once around and turns translucent; remove from heat; add:
3/4 C pineapple chunks
3/4 C lichees, cut in half
6 maraschino cherries

Heat 2 inches of oil to 400° and deep-fry chicken pieces till golden and crisp — 3 to 4 minutes; cover partially if popping is excessive. Drain on paper towels; remove bones; cut into 1-inch squares. Transfer chicken with cleaver in original shape and lay on platter. Rewarm gravy and pour over when ready to serve.

Chicken can be fried days ahead, cut up, and laid on heatproof platter ready to rewarm in 300° oven for 20 minutes. Gravy can be made ahead and rewarmed before serving.

CHICKEN AND BEAN THREADS (Long Rice)

2 C boned chicken, cut up the size of your whole thumb; remove excess skin

Mix with:
1 Tables. cornstarch
1 Tables. soy sauce
2 Tables. oil
3 to 4 slices ginger root
salt to taste

4 oz. bean threads; soak in warm water for 20 minutes to soften; cut into 4-inch lengths

1 oz. oriental mushrooms, reconstituted in 3/4 C warm water; remove stems; slice thinly; save mushroom water

1/2 C water chestnuts or bamboo shoots, sliced

1 can (11 oz.) regular-strength chicken broth with 1 Tables. sherry added

Heat 2 Tables. oil in stew pot till red hot; sauté chicken till browned; add mushrooms with their water, water chestnuts or bamboo shoots and sauté 1 minute. Add bean threads and chicken broth. Cover and simmer till most of the water is absorbed by bean threads. Bean threads should not be dried out. Garnish with slivered green onions.

Reheats well.

STEAMED CHICKEN WITH CHINESE BLACK BEANS

Put in a 1-quart heatproof bowl the following ingredients; mix and spread evenly:

    3 C boned raw chicken, cut up into pieces the size
        of your whole thumb; remove excess skin

    2 Tables. cornstarch

    1 Tables. soy sauce

    1 Tables. sherry

    1 Tables. vegetable oil

    1 to 2 teas. sugar

    salt to taste

    dash MSG

    2 Tables. fresh lemon juice

    lemon peel, cut into quarters (wash first)

    2 Tables. Chinese salted black beans; wash through
        a strainer and mince like paste with:

    2 large cloves garlic

Steam for about 30 minutes or until done, stirring once at midpoint. Remove lemon peels before serving. Taste first to adjust lemon or sugar flavor. Garnish with slivered green onions. Delicious with rice!

Variation: Lean riblets (have butcher cut up into 1-1/2-inch pieces) may be substituted for chicken. If very fat, parboil spareribs first for 2 minutes and drain; then mix with other ingredients. Add a Tables. chopped coriander before cooking, if desired.

Both can be made ahead and resteamed.

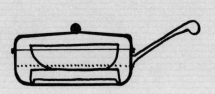

STEAMED CHICKEN WITH CHINESE SAUSAGES

Put together in a 1-quart heatproof bowl and mix:
    2 C boned chicken, cut up into pieces the size
        of your whole thumb; remove excess skin
    2 Chinese sausages; rinse under hot tap water
        1/2 minute; cut diagonally 1/4 inch thick
        and 1 inch long
    1/4 C bamboo shoots; slice thinly to match sausages
    1/4 C oriental mushrooms, reconstituted; slice thinly
    1 Tables. cornstarch
    1 Tables. soy sauce
    1 Tables. sherry
    1 Tables. oil
    3 to 4 slices ginger root
    salt to taste
    dash MSG

Spread evenly in bowl and steam for 30 minutes, turning once at midpoint. (Set the timer when water begins to boil; lower heat but keep water bubbling.)

Garnish with slivered green onions. Serve with rice.

Excellent made ahead and resteamed.

CHICKEN RICE CASSEROLE

The preceding recipe may be used to make rice casserole. Wash 2 C rice through a strainer and drain well. Put into a 4-quart saucepan; add 2 C of warm water and 1 teas. salt. Boil till the water is completely absorbed. Turn to lowest heat. Spread chicken mixture evenly over rice and steam 1/2 hour together or until done. Remove ginger slices; toss before serving.

Good reheated: add a few Tables. hot water or broth and warm on low heat 15 minutes.

FOIL-WRAPPED CHICKEN

> 3 C boned raw chicken, cut up into pieces half
> the size of your whole thumb; remove excess
> skin

Mix with:
> 1 1/2 Tables. cornstarch
> 1 Tables. soy sauce
> 1 Tables. dry sherry
> 1 Tables. Worcestershire sauce
> 1 Tables. hoisin sauce
> 3 Tables. vegetable oil
> 1/2 teas. sesame oil
> 1 small clove minced garlic
> 2 whole green onions, chopped
> salt to taste
> 1 teas. chopped fresh coriander (optional)

Have ready:
> about 24 4-1/2-inch heavy-gauge aluminum foil
> squares

Wrap 1 rounded Tables. chicken in each square; fold in triangle and then fold open edges over about 1/4 inch (arrows) to seal.　Bake single-layer in preheated 450° to 475° oven for 15 minutes or until done. (Open to check.) Flank steak may be used instead of chicken. (See p. 85 for slicing.)

This recipe is a modern version of the original Parchment Chicken which is folded in tough paper, like the kind butchers use to wrap giblets before sticking them back into the cavity of fowl. These packets, like envelopes, are then deep-fried and served immediately; they are delicious! Most hostesses do not relish last-minute deep-frying. This foil-wrapped method enables you to make them ahead to refrigerate or freeze. Thaw to room temperature before baking.

PRESSED DUCK

1 frozen duckling, 4 to 5 pounds, thawed (takes 2
    days in refrigerator)

Remove giblets; trim off extra fat. Immerse duckling completely in a pot of warm water with 1 Tables. salt and 2
whole green onions added; add giblets to pot. Cover, bring
to a boil; turn heat down to lowest point for 5 minutes — 10
minutes if duck is over 4 1/2 pounds; turn off heat. Steep
until water cools — 5 hours or more. Remove duckling and
drain; blot dry with paper towels. Smear seasoning (recipe
below) all over inside and out. Remove wings and legs;
disjoint legs; make slits along the bones; remove bones.
Leave bones in wings and discard wing tips. Use cleaver
or poultry shears to cut body of duckling into 4 quarters:
down center back and down center front and then each
piece in half. Remove bones with fingers, leaving meat in
one piece, if possible. You will have bits and pieces of
loose meat. Let air-dry for 1/2 hour.

Seasoning, mix together:
    3/4 teas. salt
    2 Tables. soy sauce
    2 Tables. sherry

While duck is drying, have ready:
    1 egg, beaten lightly

    water chestnut powder or cornstarch for dredging duck

    platter lined with finely shredded lettuce

    1/2 C chopped cocktail peanuts

Make sweet and sour sauce. In a saucepan put:

1/4 C vinegar (white or cider)
1/4 C sugar (white or brown)
2 Tables. soy sauce
2 Tables. catsup
2 Tables. cornstarch
1 C chicken broth
1 Tables. chicken-flavored soup base
few drops of Tabasco sauce
few drops of red food coloring (optional)

Stir and cook over high heat till it bubbles once around and thickens. Remove from heat and rewarm when ready to serve.

When duck has air-dried, dip sections in egg; press firmly with water chestnut powder or cornstarch; deep-fry in at least 2 inches of oil at 400° until golden and crisp — takes about 5 minutes. Meat should be done at this point because the preliminary steeping should have cooked it through except for a little pink near the bones. Lay bits and pieces on lettuce first so large pieces can cover them. Cut sections into 1- by 2-inch pieces. Transport each section in original shape (like jigsaw puzzle) over lettuce, arranging them in one gentle mound. Pour sweet and sour sauce over; top with finely chopped peanuts. You can fry the giblets and wings, but restaurants do not serve them with the duck.

Duck can be fried in the morning or day before and rewarmed in 300° oven 20 minutes and then arranged over lettuce.

Broth after steeping duck can be used for a soup base. Return other bones and add more bones to make soup, if desired. Skim off fat.

Press Duck is a misnomer in that no press is used to flatten the duck. The shape comes from the duck being boned. The Chinese name is Waw Siew Ahp.

127

CHICKEN GIZZARDS

In a saucepan, put:
- 1 pound gizzards, remove fat
- 1/2 C water
- 1/4 C soy sauce
- 1 Tables. sherry
- 2 Tables. oyster-flavored sauce
- 2 Tables. brown sugar or honey or equivalent of rock sugar
- 1 small clove garlic, minced
- pinch of five-fragrant-spices powder

Bring to a boil, cover and simmer on low heat for about 45 minutes or until liquid turns syrupy and gizzards are tender. Do not burn.

Slice lengthwise and serve warm in chafing dish as an hors d'oeuvre, using cocktail picks.

海鮮

SEA FOOD

ABALONE AND MUSHROOMS

1 can (1 pound) abalone, cut 1/8 inch
thick and 1 by 2 inches. Reserve
liquor.

1 C oriental mushrooms (p. 41), reconstituted in 1 C of water. Cut to
match abalone.

Gravy ingredients, mix together:
1/4 C liquor from abalone (save the rest for cooking)
1 Tables. cornstarch
2 Tables. oyster-flavored sauce
2 drops sesame oil
dash MSG

1/4 pound Chinese pea pods or 1/2 pound bok choy
hearts. Cut ribs in half for those bigger than your
thumb; then cut into 2-inch lengths
1 whole green onion, slivered
In a saucepan put:
mushrooms
liquor from abalone (minus 1/4 C for gravy)
1 teas. brown sugar (or rock sugar)
1 teas. lemon juice
2 to 4 Tables. vegetable oil or chicken fat
salt

Simmer 20 minutes. Add gravy ingredients and abalone.
Let bubble once around. Turn off heat.

Two minutes before adding gravy and abalone to mushrooms: Sauté and salt pea pods 1 minute or bok choy 2
minutes with 2 Tables. oil. Put on platter; spread mushrooms
and abalone over; garnish with green onions.

Mushrooms can be simmered ahead and gravy ingredients
added. Before serving, rewarm mushrooms; add abalone just to
warm through. Sauté vegetables near serving time.

SAUTÉED PRAWNS AND VEGETABLES

Cutting pattern: vegetables cut bite size to match size of prawns

1 pound large prawns—shell, devein, butterfly (p. 135).
   Soak 5 minutes with water to cover and 1 Tables.
   salt added. Rinse and drain in colander; blot with
   paper towels

1 clove garlic, smashed or minced

2 Tables. pale dry sherry

Have ready:
   1/2 C bamboo shoots
   3/4 C oriental mushrooms, reconstituted; save water for
      gravy
   1 small yellow onion
   1 stalk tender celery
   1/4 pound Chinese pea pods

Gravy ingredients, mix together:
   1 Tables. cornstarch
   1 Tables. soy sauce
   1/2 teas. MSG
   5/8 C mushroom water

Salt as needed. In sizzling hot fry pan with 3 Tables.
oil, sauté prawns till half done; add garlic and sauté until
meat turns completely from gray to white (total time less than
5 minutes); sizzle in sherry; remove from pan. Sauté bamboo
shoots and mushrooms over high heat for 1 minute; add 4
Tables. water; cover and steam 3 to 4 minutes. Add onions
and celery and sauté 1 minute; add pea pods and sauté another minute. Add mixed gravy ingredients and prawns stirring
till gravy bubbles once around.

If fresh Chinese pea pods are not available, use frozen:
thaw and separate; blot dry; cook only long enough to heat
through.

Another substitute for pea pods is green bell peppers or
frozen peas.

SAUTÉED ABALONE AND VEGETABLES

Use preceding recipe, but substitute canned abalone (1-pound size). Slice abalone 1/4 inch thick and 1 inch by 2 inches. Use abalone liquid to make gravy instead of water from mushrooms; add 2 Tables. oyster-flavored sauce to gravy ingredients. Sauté vegetables as directed; add mixed gravy ingredients and abalone; stir till gravy bubbles once around. Abalone comes cooked in the can; it needs only to warm through; further cooking toughens it.

If fresh abalone is used, pound prodigiously, slice thinly and sauté briefly with oil and garlic; then sizzle with sherry, same as for prawns.

SAUTÉED SQUID AND VEGETABLES

Clean squid and cut into 1-inch by 2-inch pieces. Blot completely dry and proceed same as for prawns.

SHRIMP AND BEAN SPROUT SALAD

1 pound fresh bean sprouts, wash and drain
Put in a bowl and toss with:
    1 Tables. sugar
    1 Tables. lemon juice

Add:
    1 can (11 oz.) mandarin oranges or 1 can
       (1 pound) pineapple chunks, drained

    1 C cooked salad shrimp or crab meat

    1 carton (8 oz.) pineapple-flavored yogurt; mix with:
    1 teas. or less curry powder
    1 Tables. soy sauce

Toss all together just before serving. Sprinkle with:
    1/2 C chopped cocktail peanuts

SAUTÉED PRAWNS OVER SIZZLE RICE

6 strips bacon

1 pound large prawns — shell, devein, butterfly.
  Cover with water and add 1 Tables. salt;
  soak 5 minutes; rinse and drain well in
  colander
1 clove garlic, smashed

2 Tables. sherry

1 bell pepper, cut bite size (p. 13)
1 yellow onion cut the same

Gravy ingredients, mix together in bowl:
  3/4 C chicken broth
  1 Tables. cornstarch
  2 Tables. catsup
  1 Tables. Worcestershire sauce
  1 Tables. soy sauce
  1/2 teas. or less Tabasco sauce

Deep-fry; break up and lay on a platter; keep warm in 200°
oven:
  1 recipe sizzle rice (see Sizzle Rice Soup, p. 72)

Brown bacon on both sides in fry pan on medium heat.
Cut into 1-inch pieces; drain on paper towels. Leave 1 Tables.
oil in pan. Salt and sauté peppers and onions 1 to 2 minutes,
adding 1 Tables. water; remove from pan. Heat fry pan red
hot; add 3 Tables. bacon grease or vegetable oil; sear prawns
till half done — about 2 minutes; add garlic, sauté till done;
sizzle in sherry. Return vegetables and bacon; add mixed
gravy ingredients; stir and let bubble once around. Serve over
sizzle rice.

TO SHELL, DEVEIN, AND BUTTERFLY PRAWNS

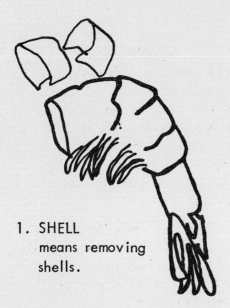

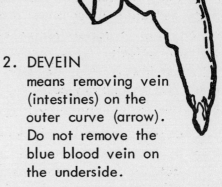

1. SHELL means removing shells.

2. DEVEIN means removing vein (intestines) on the outer curve (arrow). Do not remove the blue blood vein on the underside.

3. BUTTERFLY means cutting deeper. Devein and butterfly in one step.

4. FOR DEEP-FRIED PRAWNS Leave shell tails on. They serve as attractive handles.

135

DEEP-FRIED BUTTERFLY PRAWNS

   1 pound large prawns, butterflied,
       leave tails on (p. 135)

   Barely cover prawns with cold water
to which 1 Tables. salt has been added; soak 10 minutes.
Rinse and drain in colander and then blot dry on paper
towels. Dip in batter (recipe below) and deep-fry in 400°
oil until golden — takes about 2 minutes. Drain single-layer
on paper towels. May be kept warm in oven until serving
time. Dip in mustard paste (p. 42), Sweet and Sour Sauce
(p. 116), or Cocktail Sauce (p. 116).

   Soaking prawns in salt water improves their flavor, gives
them a firmer texture, and draws water from them so they do
not create steam to soften the crust when battered and deep-
fried. The ice water used in the batter makes it cold so it
fluffs more when "surprised" by the hot oil.

BUTTERFLY PRAWNS BATTER

Mix together lightly; leave lumps in:
   1 C cornstarch
   1 C Bisquick
   1 C ice water, approximately. Add slowly near end
       until you get a consistency like pancake batter
       or thinner
   2 drops of yellow food coloring. This gives the batter
       an "eggy" look. Prawns take only 2 minutes to cook
       and much longer to brown when fresh oil is used. It
       is bad policy to prolong cooking the prawns for the
       purpose of browning as the oil breaks down with
       hard use.

Preparation ahead: Prepare and drain the day before. The day
of party: Deep-fry hours ahead without refrigerating. Rewarm
single-layer, uncovered, in 300° oven 10 to 15 minutes.

136

SAUTÉED PRAWNS IN THE SHELL

 1 pound large raw prawns, deveined through shell by
  using serrated knife. Soak 5 minutes in water with
  1 Tables. salt added; rinse and drain in colander
  first; blot dry on paper towels

 1 large clove garlic, smashed or minced

 4 Tables. pale dry sherry
 2 Tables. soy sauce

 2 whole green onions, cut into 1/4-inch pieces

Heat fry pan till red hot with 4 Tables. oil and sear
prawns till half done — about 2 minutes. Salt and add garlic
and finish cooking, covering and lowering heat if necessary
to prevent scorching. Sizzle in sherry and soy sauce; add
green onions and sauté once around. Serve on warmed platter.
Garnish with parsley if desired.

Chinese relish eating sea food in the shell for its flavor.
You may use fingers to assist. This dish can be done without
the shells, if preferred.

Prawns may be deveined and drained the day before.

SWEET AND SOUR FISH

1 to 1 1/4 pounds fish fillets
(red snappers or rock cod),
salted, peppered, moistened
with beaten egg and dredged
in cornstarch or flour

2 cloves garlic, minced
1 knob ginger root (size of your thumb),
peeled and sliced

1/4 C pale dry sherry

1/2 yellow onion, cut into bite-size pieces
1/2 bell pepper — cut into bite-size pieces
1 tomato, skinned and cut into 6ths or 8ths

1 small can pineapple chunks (15 oz.) drained,
save juice for gravy

Gravy ingredients, mix together:
juice from pineapple — 5/8 C (1/2 C + 2 Tables.)
1 Tables. catsup
1 Tables. soy sauce
1 Tables. sugar (brown or white)
1 Tables. cider vinegar (or other)
1 1/2 Tables. cornstarch

Heat 2 Tables. oil in fry pan till hot; brown fish fillets
on one side, spreading garlic and ginger over and around
fish. Turn and brown other side; cover to cook through; turn
down heat if necessary to prevent scorching. Remove garlic
and ginger if they burn; add more oil as needed. It takes
about 5 to 10 minutes to cook fish, depending on the
thickness. Poke through thickest part to check for doneness;
sizzle in sherry; transfer to warmed platter.

Wipe clean fry pan; heat about 3 Tables. oil and sauté
onions, bell peppers and tomatoes until half done — about 1
minute. Add pineapples and stirred gravy ingredients; stir till
thickened. Spread over fish.

138

SUB GUM FISH

Cutting pattern: vegetables (except tomato) and sub gum are cut into thin strips.

1 1/4 pound fish fillets — rock cod or red snapper; season with salt and pepper; moisten with beaten egg; dredge in flour

6 slices ginger root
2 cloves garlic, smashed or minced

2 Tables. or more sherry

1 tomato, skin and cut into eighths
1 stalk tender celery
1 small round onion

1/2 can (1 1/2 pound) sub gum; reserve brine for gravy

Gravy ingredients, mix together:
1 Tables. cornstarch
1 Tables. soy sauce
1 Tables. catsup
1/2 C brine from sub gum and 1/4 C water

In hot fry pan with 4 Tables. oil lay fish fillets without agitating, spreading ginger and garlic on top and around. Brown one side; turn and brown the other. Turn heat down, covering if necessary to cook through — takes 5 to 10 minutes depending on thickness of fillets. Remove garlic and ginger; sizzle in sherry; transfer fillets to warmed platter. Wipe pan clean; sauté tomatoes, celery and onions about 2 minutes; add sub gum and mixed gravy ingredients and stir until thickened; spread over fillets.

Chinese serve fish whole complete with heads. Each diner digs out his own portion. For American-style dining, cut fish up into serving-size portions.

SHRIMP CURRY — Chinese-Style

1 pound raw prawns — shell, devein and halve lengthwise, wash and drain on paper towels.

1 clove garlic, smashed or minced
3 slices peeled, fresh ginger root, size of quarters

Seasonings, combine in a bowl and set aside:
   1 to 2 Tables. curry powder
   2 Tables. dry sherry
   1 Tables. soy sauce
   1 Tables. Worcestershire sauce
   few drops Tabasco sauce or any hot chili sauce

Dice into 1/2-inch cubes the following vegetables and combine in a bowl:
   1 small stalk celery
   1/2 yellow onion
   1/2 bell pepper
   1 pippin apple, peel first

   2 cans cream of mushroom soup, undiluted

Do not salt as mushroom soup is used undiluted. Sauté
vegetables all together with 2 Tables. oil for 2 minutes.
Remove from pan.

Sauté prawns, garlic and ginger slices over high heat
with 3 Tables. oil till prawns turn from gray to white. Add
seasonings and sauté once around. Return vegetables to pan;
mix in mushroom soup; turn to lowest heat and warm to eating
temperature only. Serve with rice.

Accompany with any or all of these: tomato slices,
chopped cocktail peanuts, shredded coconut, chutney,

pineapple chunks, mandarin oranges, bananas, chopped hard-cooked eggs, bacon crumbles.

Shrimp curry is not a Chinese recipe, but the sautéed method of quick cooking is.

To make ahead: Add mushroom soup; remove from heat. Keeps 3 to 4 days refrigerated. Heat slowly to warm through; do not prolong heating as it toughens prawns.

Suggestion for a large crowd. Accompany with baked ham and a green salad — easy!

NAPPA CABBAGE WITH CRAB MEAT SAUCE

        1 1/2 pounds Nappa cabbage (p. 42), cut
            across into 1-inch widths
        3 slices peeled ginger root
        1/2 pound cooked crab meat

Sauce ingredients, mix together:
        3/4 C chicken broth
        1 Tables. chicken-flavored soup base
        1 Tables. cornstarch
        1 Tables. soy sauce (light preferred)

In medium-hot fry pan with 2 Tables. oil sauté cabbage with ginger slices and salt till translucent. Drain off excess liquid; remove ginger slices. Transfer cabbage to warmed platter. Drain liquid again before adding sauce over.

Stir and cook sauce ingredients till thickened. Add crab meat chunks and warm through. Spread over cabbage.

Variation: Cream Sauce
        1 C light cream (half-and-half)
        1 Tables. butter
        1 Tables. cornstarch
        1 Tables. chicken-flavored soup base

LOBSTERS AND BLACK BEAN SAUCE
(Cantonese Lobster)

2 to 3 lobster tails (total about 1 pound), thaw completely

1. With kitchen shears remove swimmerets and membrane from under side (along dotted lines); leave shells on.

2. Cut across tails into 1-inch chunks, using cleaver or shears; drain well on paper towels.

1 pork chop, mince like hamburger
2 Tables. Chinese salted black beans; wash through a strainer and <u>mince like paste</u> with:
2 large cloves garlic

2 Tables. sherry

1 bell pepper, cut bite size
1 yellow onion, cut bite size

Gravy ingredients, mix together:
    1 Tables. cornstarch
    1 Tables. soy sauce
    3/4 C chicken broth

1 egg white slightly beaten

Salt as needed. Sauté peppers and onions over medium-high heat with 2 Tables. oil for 1 minute; remove from pan. Over high heat with 4 Tables. oil brown lobster pieces on one side without agitating; turn to brown one other side, adding pork, black beans and garlic in between lobster pieces and stirring to prevent scorching. When pork has browned lightly, sizzle in sherry; lower heat; add 2 Tables. water; cover to finish cooking lobster pieces — meat turns from gray to white. Return vegetables and mixed gravy ingredients; toss till thickened. Add egg white and stir once around so it cooks in flecks. Do not overhandle!

If 1-pound tails are used, cut lengthwise down the middle first before cutting into chunks.

Agitate as little as possible to keep meat in shells. Shells give flavor and a bright red color to the dish. You may shell the tails, sacrificing drama and flavor for convenience; 1/4 cup pimiento added would restore color to this dish.

For a zesty hot dish: Fresh chili peppers may be sliced and sautéed along with the garlic and black beans.

Prawns or cracked crab may be substituted for lobster tails; or use half prawns and half lobster tails to stretch the latter.

SHRIMP TOAST

Spread: cut up the following and then mince together like paste:

    1/2 pound raw prawns — shell
        and devein
    1 strip bacon or equivalent of
        ham or barbecued pork on
        fat side
    1/4 C jicama or water chestnuts (or celery)
    1 whole green onion
    1 teas. fresh coriander leaves (optional)

Mix with:
    2 teas. cornstarch
    2 teas. soy sauce
    2 teas. sherry
    few drops of sesame oil
    1/4 teas. MSG
    salt and pepper

Have ready:
    6 pieces or more stale sandwich bread (3 to 4 days old —
        absorbs less oil); trim off crust

Spread mixture evenly on bread, covering entire surface. Wet cleaver each time in cold water (to prevent sticking) and cut bread into 4 triangles. Deep-fry 375° with 2 inches oil with meat side down until golden and done — about 1 minute; it is not necessary to turn them. To cut oil absorption on bread: Use only enough oil to fry shrimp portion — about 1/2 inch or less. Drain on paper towels. May be reheated in oven. Freezing not recommended. Good as an hors d'oeuvre or with Coriander Chicken Salad.

甜品

SWEETS

146

TEEM GAWK

Teem Gawk translated means sweet turnover. This confection uses a wun tun wrapper and the filling below and is then deep-fried.

1 pound wun tun wrappers

Filling, mix together:
   1/2 C chopped (like oatmeal) cocktail peanuts (not Spanish peanuts)
   1/2 C white or brown sugar (packed)
   1/2 C angel flake coconut (fine cut)
   1/4 C sesame seeds
   1 Tables. lightly beaten egg (reserve the rest for sealing edges)

Hold a wrapper in palm of your left hand; moisten edges all around with egg, using your right forefinger. Spoon about 1 Tables. filling in center of wrapper without getting any on the edges. Fold into triangle and pinch edges together hard to get a tight seal. Wrap about 15 of these at a time without piling them on top of each other as they may stick. Check seal and deep-fry in 1 to 2 inches of oil at 375° on both sides until golden. Drain single-layer on paper towels. Sift powdered sugar over if desired. Continue to wrap until filling is used up. Have a fine-gauge strainer handy to skim off bits of filling if edges open. It is easiest to have one person wrap and one person deep-fry.

Eat warm or cool and store in airtight container. Keeps like potato chips. Leftover wun tun wrappers can be made into Dahn Sahn (recipe follows).

If available, suay gow pay instead of wun tun wrappers are usually used for turnovers, so you have a half circle rather than a triangle.

Try this filling: 1/4 C chopped dried apricot or raisins, 1/4 C chopped walnuts, 1/4 C coconut, 1/4 C brown sugar. Make up your own!

MINIATURE DAHN SAHN

Dahn Sahn means egg fluff. It is a pastry shaped like a bow, usually 3 by 6 inches, deep-fried and sweetened with a syrup. This recipe is an easy miniature version using wun tun dough (a good way to use leftovers). Shape as illustrated. Deep-fry at 375° on both sides for one minute or until golden. Drain single-layer. Drizzle with pancake syrup, honey, or Caramel Syrup (recipe follows). Serve hot or cold.

Suggestion: For children, serve as you would caramel popcorn or cotton candy in paper cups. Send them outdoors!

TO SHAPE DAHN SAHN

Cut a stack of wun tun dough in half with cleaver.

Line up 2 halves; slit 3/4 inch at center. Pull one end through slit in direction of arrow so you have a bow like . . .

. . . this.

CARAMEL SYRUP

Use to drizzle over Dahn Sahn.

    1 1/2 Tables. butter
    1 C white sugar
    1/2 C brown sugar
    1/4 teas. cream of tartar
    6 Tables. water

Stir to dissolve sugar and bring to a boil. Cover and cook about 3 minutes until steam washes down crystals on

148

sides of pan. Uncover and cook without stirring to the soft-ball stage, 240°.

For Candied Ginger Syrup: Add 1/4 C minced candied ginger with other ingredients.

GINGER SUNDAE SAUCE

In a saucepan put:
    2 C granulated sugar
    3/4 C water
    1/4 teas. cream of tartar
    1/4 C finely chopped candied ginger

Simmer 5 minutes and remove from heat.

Add:
    1 Tables. lemon juice
    1 drop yellow coloring
    1/2 C light cream

For caramel flavor, add:
    2 Tables. butter

Makes 1 3/4 cups.

Serve over lemon sherbet, vanilla ice cream or sponge cake.

GINGER ICE CREAM

Make your own: Soften one quart of vanilla ice cream and mix in about 1/4 C or less of finely chopped candied ginger and refreeze.

STEAMED SPONGE CAKE

Put into a 1-1/2-quart mixing bowl:
    3 eggs
    3/4 C granulated sugar

Beat 5 minutes on high speed until creamy. Add:
    1/2 teas. vanilla and 1/2 teas. almond extract
    3/4 C sifted cake flour

Blend on low speed for 3 to 5 minutes until smooth. Pour into 9-inch round cake pan with bottom lined. Put in steamer with water gently bubbling for 15 minutes or until knife comes out clean when inserted in the center of cake. Cake can be left in pan to keep warm (drain off water from lid). May be eaten cold or rewarmed in steam. To remove cake from pan: run spatula around the sides; invert pan over wax paper and tap bottom of pan. Peel off wax paper. Cut cake into wedges.
    Delicious with Orange Ginger Sauce or Ginger Whipped Cream with mandarin oranges.

ORANGE GINGER SAUCE

Combine in a 1-quart saucepan:
    1 can frozen orange juice (6 oz.)
    1 teas. grated lemon peel
    2 Tables. lemon juice
    1/2 C sugar (brown or white)
    1 1/2 Tables. cornstarch
    1 Tables. or more chopped candied ginger
    juice from 1 can mandarin oranges (11 oz.)

Stir and cook over medium high heat till it bubbles once around. Remove from heat; add oranges. Serve warm over vanilla ice cream or sponge cake.

GINGER WHIPPED CREAM

Whip until thick:
    1/2 pint cream

Blend in:
    1/2 teas. vanilla
    2 Tables. powdered sugar
    1 Tables. finely chopped candied ginger

Enough for one layer sponge cake.

ALMOND VELVET PUDDING

    1 envelope gelatine, dissolved in:
    2 Tables. cold water

    7/8 C (1 C minus 2 Tables.) boiling water
    1/4 C white sugar
    1 C evaporated milk or light cream (half-and-half) or
        concentrated milk (undiluted)
    1 1/2 to 2 teas. almond extract
    few drops of red food coloring

    1 can (10 oz.) lichees; cut lichees in half; refrigerate
        with syrup to which 2 Tables. maraschino cherry
        juice and 2 drops of almond extract have been
        added

Add boiling water to gelatine paste and stir until dis-
solved. Add sugar, milk, a few drops of food coloring and
almond extract. Pour into an 8-inch square pan and refrigerate
until firm. Dice into 1/2-inch cubes. Add chilled canned
lichees with syrup; pile gently into sherbet glasses;
garnish with maraschino cherries.

Variation: Diced watermelon or mandarin oranges may
be added.

ALMOND COOKIES

1 C Crisco or lard
1 C granulated sugar or brown sugar (or 1/2 C each)
1 egg
2 1/4 C sifted all-purpose flour
1 teas. baking soda
1/8 teas. salt
1 1/2 teas. almond extract

blanched almonds

Cream Crisco with sugar; add egg and mix well. Add dry ingredients which have been sifted together; mix; add almond extract. Shape into balls about 1 inch in diameter; place on ungreased baking sheet with ample space between to allow for expansion. Press an almond in center of each ball and bake at 375° for 15 minutes.

For sesame cookies, roll ball all around with seeds and bake. Makes 4 to 5 dozen.

FRUIT COMPOTE À L'ORIENTALE

Combine in a large bowl and chill:
    canned mandarin oranges, drained
    canned loongans, drained
    canned lichees, with juice
    canned pineapple chunks, with juice
    melon balls
    fresh strawberries (halve large ones), sugar first
    fresh grapes, sugar first
    any fruit in season

If bananas or fresh pears are used, put in just before serving to prevent discoloring. Sprinkle with chopped candied ginger and garnish with mint leaves.

After a heavy Chinese dinner, fruit provides a light finale.

SHOPPING GUIDE

American Name	Ask For	Chinese Name
Abalone, Canned	Bow Yue	罐頭鮑魚
Bamboo Shoots	Jook Suen	竹筍
Bean, (Soy) Cake	Dow Foo	豆腐
Bean Sauce	Mein See Jeong	原晒豉醬
Bean Threads	Fun See	粉絲
Black Beans, Salted	Dow See	豆豉
Cabbage, Celery or Nappa	Siew (rhymes with "view") Choy	兆菜
Cabbage, Chinese	Bok Choy	白菜
Egg Roll Wrappers	Cheun Guen Pay	春捲皮
Fuzzy Melon (Squash)	Mo Gwa	毛瓜
Ginger, Fresh	Sahng Geung	生羌
Hoisin Sauce	Hoi Seen Jeong	海鮮醬
Long Beans, Chinese	Dow Gawk	荳角
Mushrooms, Dried	Doong Gwoo	冬菇
Oyster-Flavored Sauce	Ho Yow	蠔油

American Name	Ask For	Chinese Name
Rice Sticks	Pie Mai Fun	排米粉
Sesame Oil	Jee Mah Yow	蔴油
Snow Peas	Haw Lon Dow	荷蘭豆
Spice Powder (Five Spices	Heung Liew Fun (rhymes with "view")	香料分
Suay Gow Wrappers	Suay Gow Pay	水餃皮
Sub Gum (Mix, Ginger and Vegetables)	Sub Gum	什錦慈
Tangerine Peel, Dried	Gwaw Pay	菓皮
Turnip, Dried	Choong Choy	冲菜
Vinegar, Chinese	Chit Cho	浙醋
Water Chestnuts	Ma Tai	馬蹄
Winter Melon	Doong Gwa	冬瓜
Wun Tun Wrappers	Wun Tun Pay	雲吞皮

ORDER FORM

To order extra copies of YOUR FAVORITE RECIPES fill in Order Form below or a facsimile. Send with check or money order for $4.50 each ($3.50 plus $1.00 to cover sales tax, postage within U.S., and handling charges) to:

Lily Chinn
753 Peekskill Drive
Sunnyvale, CA 94087

- -

To:
Lily Chinn
753 Peekskill Drive
Sunnyvale, CA 94087

Please send me _____ copies of YOUR FAVORITE RECIPES.

I enclose $_____ ___ check
                       ___ money order

(Please print)

_____
Name

_____
Address

_____
City   State   Zip